50 Homemade Casserole Recipes for Home

By: Kelly Johnson

Table of Contents

- Classic Tater Tot Casserole
- Cheesy Chicken and Broccoli Casserole
- Beef and Mushroom Stroganoff Casserole
- Spinach and Artichoke Breakfast Casserole
- Mexican Quinoa Casserole
- Zucchini and Tomato Gratin
- Turkey and Wild Rice Casserole
- Sweet Potato and Black Bean Enchilada Casserole
- Sausage and Egg Breakfast Casserole
- Mediterranean Eggplant Casserole
- Chicken Alfredo Pasta Bake
- Cheesy Potato Casserole
- Egg and Veggie Breakfast Casserole
- Italian Sausage and Pasta Casserole
- Vegan Lentil Shepherd's Pie
- Chicken Parmesan Casserole
- Baked Macaroni and Cheese Casserole
- Hawaiian Pineapple Chicken Casserole
- Cauliflower and Broccoli Gratin
- Beef and Potato Hash Brown Casserole
- Chicken and Rice Casserole
- Sausage and Spinach Breakfast Casserole
- Vegetable Lasagna Casserole
- Tex-Mex Beef Enchilada Casserole
- Greek Moussaka Casserole
- Breakfast Burrito Casserole
- Creamy Spinach and Mushroom Pasta Bake
- Mexican Chicken Tortilla Casserole
- Butternut Squash and Kale Quinoa Casserole
- Baked Spaghetti Squash Casserole
- Buffalo Chicken Pasta Bake
- Broccoli and Cheese Quiche Casserole
- Italian Meatball Casserole
- Vegetarian Chili Cornbread Casserole
- Chicken and Stuffing Casserole

- Ratatouille Casserole
- Beefy Taco Casserole
- Corn and Green Chile Breakfast Casserole
- Cheesy Broccoli and Rice Casserole
- Creamy Chicken and Mushroom Casserole
- Vegetarian Eggplant Parmesan Casserole
- Sloppy Joe Tater Tot Casserole
- Turkey and Cranberry Casserole
- Mexican Beef and Rice Casserole
- Breakfast Sausage and Potato Casserole
- Spinach and Feta Pasta Bake
- BBQ Pulled Pork Mac and Cheese Casserole
- Chicken and Dumplings Casserole
- Mediterranean Chickpea Casserole
- Veggie and Quinoa Breakfast Casserole

Classic Tater Tot Casserole

Ingredients:

- 1 pound ground beef
- 1 small onion, diced
- 1 can (10.75 ounces) condensed cream of mushroom soup
- 1/2 cup milk
- 2 cups shredded cheddar cheese
- 1 package (32 ounces) frozen Tater Tots
- Salt and pepper to taste

Instructions:

1. Preheat your oven to 375°F (190°C).
2. In a skillet over medium heat, cook the ground beef and diced onion until the beef is browned and the onion is softened. Drain any excess fat.
3. In a mixing bowl, combine the condensed cream of mushroom soup and milk. Stir until smooth.
4. Add the cooked ground beef and diced onion to the soup mixture. Season with salt and pepper to taste. Stir until well combined.
5. Spread the beef and soup mixture evenly into the bottom of a 9x13-inch baking dish.
6. Sprinkle the shredded cheddar cheese over the beef mixture.
7. Arrange the frozen Tater Tots in a single layer on top of the cheese, covering the entire surface of the casserole.
8. Bake in the preheated oven for 30-35 minutes, or until the Tater Tots are golden brown and crispy and the casserole is bubbly around the edges.
9. Remove from the oven and let it cool for a few minutes before serving.
10. Serve the classic Tater Tot Casserole warm and enjoy!

This classic Tater Tot Casserole is a comforting and hearty dish that's perfect for a family dinner or potluck gathering. It's simple to make and always a hit with both kids and adults alike!

Cheesy Chicken and Broccoli Casserole

Ingredients:

- 2 cups cooked chicken, shredded or cubed
- 3 cups broccoli florets, steamed or blanched
- 1 can (10.75 oz) condensed cream of chicken soup
- 1/2 cup mayonnaise
- 1/2 cup sour cream
- 1 cup shredded cheddar cheese, divided
- 1/2 cup grated Parmesan cheese
- 1 tablespoon Dijon mustard
- 1 teaspoon garlic powder
- Salt and pepper to taste
- 2 cups cooked rice or pasta (optional)
- 1/2 cup breadcrumbs (optional)
- 2 tablespoons melted butter (optional)

Instructions:

1. Preheat your oven to 350°F (175°C). Grease a 9x13-inch baking dish with butter or cooking spray.
2. In a large mixing bowl, combine the condensed cream of chicken soup, mayonnaise, sour cream, half of the shredded cheddar cheese, grated Parmesan cheese, Dijon mustard, garlic powder, salt, and pepper. Mix well until smooth and creamy.
3. Add the cooked chicken and steamed broccoli florets to the bowl with the sauce mixture. Stir until everything is well coated.
4. If using cooked rice or pasta, add it to the mixture and stir until evenly combined.
5. Transfer the mixture to the prepared baking dish and spread it out evenly.
6. Sprinkle the remaining shredded cheddar cheese over the top of the casserole.
7. If desired, mix the breadcrumbs with melted butter and sprinkle them over the cheese layer for added crunch.
8. Bake in the preheated oven for 25-30 minutes, or until the cheese is melted and bubbly, and the casserole is heated through.
9. Remove from the oven and let it cool for a few minutes before serving.
10. Serve the cheesy chicken and broccoli casserole warm and enjoy!

This cheesy chicken and broccoli casserole is a comforting and satisfying dish that's perfect for a family dinner or potluck gathering. It's easy to make and packed with flavor, making it a favorite among both kids and adults alike!

Beef and Mushroom Stroganoff Casserole

Ingredients:

- 1 pound ground beef
- 1 onion, finely chopped
- 2 cloves garlic, minced
- 8 ounces mushrooms, sliced
- 1 can (10.75 ounces) condensed cream of mushroom soup
- 1 cup beef broth
- 1 cup sour cream
- 1 tablespoon Worcestershire sauce
- 1 teaspoon Dijon mustard
- Salt and pepper to taste
- 8 ounces egg noodles, cooked according to package instructions
- 1 cup shredded mozzarella cheese
- 1/4 cup chopped fresh parsley (optional, for garnish)

Instructions:

1. Preheat your oven to 375°F (190°C). Grease a 9x13-inch baking dish with butter or cooking spray.
2. In a large skillet, cook the ground beef over medium heat until browned. Drain any excess fat.
3. Add the chopped onion to the skillet and cook until softened, about 3-4 minutes. Add the minced garlic and sliced mushrooms, and cook for an additional 5 minutes, or until the mushrooms are tender.
4. Stir in the condensed cream of mushroom soup, beef broth, sour cream, Worcestershire sauce, Dijon mustard, salt, and pepper. Mix until well combined and heated through.
5. Add the cooked egg noodles to the skillet and toss to coat them in the sauce mixture.
6. Transfer the beef and mushroom mixture to the prepared baking dish and spread it out evenly.
7. Sprinkle the shredded mozzarella cheese over the top of the casserole.
8. Bake in the preheated oven for 20-25 minutes, or until the cheese is melted and bubbly.

9. Remove from the oven and let it cool for a few minutes before serving.
10. Garnish with chopped fresh parsley, if desired, and serve the beef and mushroom stroganoff casserole warm.

This beef and mushroom stroganoff casserole is a comforting and hearty dish that's perfect for a family dinner or potluck gathering. It's easy to make and packed with rich and savory flavors that everyone will love!

Spinach and Artichoke Breakfast Casserole

Ingredients:

- 1 tablespoon olive oil
- 1 small onion, finely chopped
- 2 cloves garlic, minced
- 8 ounces fresh spinach, roughly chopped
- 1 can (14 ounces) artichoke hearts, drained and chopped
- 6 large eggs
- 1 cup milk (any kind you prefer)
- 1/2 cup grated Parmesan cheese
- 1 cup shredded mozzarella cheese
- Salt and pepper to taste
- Dash of nutmeg (optional)
- Cooking spray or butter for greasing

Instructions:

1. Preheat your oven to 375°F (190°C). Grease a 9x13-inch baking dish with cooking spray or butter.
2. In a large skillet, heat the olive oil over medium heat. Add the chopped onion and cook until softened, about 3-4 minutes. Add the minced garlic and cook for another 1-2 minutes until fragrant.
3. Add the chopped spinach to the skillet and cook until wilted, stirring occasionally, about 3-4 minutes.
4. Stir in the chopped artichoke hearts and cook for another 2 minutes. Remove from heat and let cool slightly.
5. In a mixing bowl, whisk together the eggs, milk, grated Parmesan cheese, shredded mozzarella cheese, salt, pepper, and nutmeg (if using).
6. Stir the cooked spinach and artichoke mixture into the egg mixture until well combined.
7. Pour the mixture into the prepared baking dish and spread it out evenly.
8. Bake in the preheated oven for 25-30 minutes, or until the casserole is set and the top is golden brown.
9. Remove from the oven and let it cool for a few minutes before slicing and serving.

10. Serve the spinach and artichoke breakfast casserole warm, garnished with additional grated Parmesan cheese or fresh herbs if desired.

This spinach and artichoke breakfast casserole is a flavorful and nutritious way to start your day. It's packed with protein and veggies, making it a satisfying and delicious meal for breakfast or brunch!

Mexican Quinoa Casserole

Ingredients:

- 1 cup quinoa, rinsed
- 1 tablespoon olive oil
- 1 onion, diced
- 2 cloves garlic, minced
- 1 bell pepper, diced
- 1 can (15 ounces) black beans, drained and rinsed
- 1 cup corn kernels (fresh, frozen, or canned)
- 1 can (15 ounces) diced tomatoes, drained
- 1 cup salsa
- 1 tablespoon chili powder
- 1 teaspoon ground cumin
- 1 teaspoon paprika
- Salt and pepper to taste
- 1 cup shredded cheddar cheese
- Fresh cilantro, chopped (for garnish)
- Avocado slices (for garnish)
- Sour cream or Greek yogurt (optional, for serving)

Instructions:

1. Preheat your oven to 375°F (190°C). Grease a 9x13-inch baking dish with cooking spray or olive oil.
2. In a large skillet, heat the olive oil over medium heat. Add the diced onion and cook until softened, about 3-4 minutes. Add the minced garlic and diced bell pepper, and cook for another 2-3 minutes until fragrant.
3. Add the rinsed quinoa to the skillet and toast it for 1-2 minutes, stirring frequently.
4. Stir in the drained black beans, corn kernels, diced tomatoes, salsa, chili powder, ground cumin, paprika, salt, and pepper. Mix well to combine.
5. Transfer the quinoa mixture to the prepared baking dish and spread it out evenly.
6. Cover the baking dish with aluminum foil and bake in the preheated oven for 25 minutes.

7. Remove the foil and sprinkle the shredded cheddar cheese over the top of the casserole.
8. Return the casserole to the oven and bake, uncovered, for an additional 10-15 minutes, or until the cheese is melted and bubbly.
9. Remove from the oven and let it cool for a few minutes before serving.
10. Garnish the Mexican quinoa casserole with chopped fresh cilantro and avocado slices.
11. Serve warm, with sour cream or Greek yogurt on the side if desired.

This Mexican quinoa casserole is a flavorful and nutritious meal that's perfect for a weeknight dinner or for entertaining guests. It's packed with protein, fiber, and veggies, making it a satisfying and delicious option for any occasion!

Zucchini and Tomato Gratin

Ingredients:

- 2 large zucchinis, thinly sliced
- 2 large tomatoes, thinly sliced
- 2 cloves garlic, minced
- 1/4 cup fresh basil leaves, chopped
- 1/4 cup grated Parmesan cheese
- 1/4 cup breadcrumbs
- 2 tablespoons olive oil
- Salt and pepper to taste

Instructions:

1. Preheat your oven to 375°F (190°C). Grease a 9x13-inch baking dish with olive oil or cooking spray.
2. Arrange the sliced zucchinis and tomatoes in the prepared baking dish, alternating between them and overlapping slightly.
3. Sprinkle the minced garlic and chopped fresh basil evenly over the zucchini and tomato slices.
4. In a small bowl, mix together the grated Parmesan cheese, breadcrumbs, and olive oil until well combined.
5. Sprinkle the breadcrumb mixture evenly over the top of the zucchini and tomato slices.
6. Season the gratin with salt and pepper to taste.
7. Cover the baking dish with aluminum foil and bake in the preheated oven for 25-30 minutes, or until the vegetables are tender.
8. Remove the foil and bake for an additional 10-15 minutes, or until the top is golden brown and crispy.
9. Remove from the oven and let it cool for a few minutes before serving.
10. Serve the zucchini and tomato gratin warm as a delicious side dish or as a light vegetarian main course.

This zucchini and tomato gratin is a flavorful and colorful dish that's perfect for showcasing summer produce. It's easy to make and pairs well with a variety of main dishes. Enjoy!

Turkey and Wild Rice Casserole

Ingredients:

- 1 cup uncooked wild rice
- 2 cups chicken broth (or vegetable broth)
- 1 tablespoon olive oil
- 1 onion, chopped
- 2 cloves garlic, minced
- 2 celery stalks, chopped
- 2 carrots, diced
- 2 cups cooked turkey, shredded or diced
- 1 cup frozen peas
- 1 cup sliced mushrooms
- 1/2 cup chopped fresh parsley
- 1 teaspoon dried thyme
- Salt and pepper to taste
- 1 cup shredded cheddar cheese (optional)

For the sauce:

- 4 tablespoons butter
- 1/4 cup all-purpose flour
- 2 cups milk (any kind you prefer)
- 1/2 teaspoon salt
- 1/4 teaspoon black pepper
- 1/4 teaspoon paprika

Instructions:

1. Preheat your oven to 375°F (190°C). Grease a 9x13-inch baking dish with cooking spray or butter.
2. In a medium saucepan, combine the wild rice and chicken broth. Bring to a boil over medium-high heat. Reduce the heat to low, cover, and simmer for 45-50 minutes, or until the rice is tender and the liquid is absorbed. Remove from heat and set aside.

3. In a large skillet, heat the olive oil over medium heat. Add the chopped onion, minced garlic, celery, and carrots. Cook, stirring occasionally, for about 5 minutes, or until the vegetables are softened.
4. Add the cooked turkey, frozen peas, sliced mushrooms, chopped parsley, and dried thyme to the skillet. Season with salt and pepper to taste. Cook for an additional 3-4 minutes, or until the turkey is heated through and the vegetables are tender.
5. In a separate saucepan, melt the butter over medium heat. Stir in the flour and cook for 1-2 minutes, stirring constantly, until the mixture is smooth and bubbly.
6. Gradually whisk in the milk until smooth. Cook, stirring constantly, until the sauce thickens, about 5-7 minutes.
7. Stir in the salt, pepper, and paprika. Remove from heat.
8. In a large mixing bowl, combine the cooked wild rice, turkey and vegetable mixture, and the prepared sauce. Mix until well combined.
9. Transfer the mixture to the prepared baking dish and spread it out evenly.
10. If desired, sprinkle the shredded cheddar cheese over the top of the casserole.
11. Cover the baking dish with aluminum foil and bake in the preheated oven for 25-30 minutes, or until heated through and bubbly.
12. Remove the foil and bake for an additional 5-10 minutes, or until the cheese is melted and golden brown.
13. Remove from the oven and let it cool for a few minutes before serving.
14. Serve the turkey and wild rice casserole warm, garnished with additional chopped parsley if desired.

This turkey and wild rice casserole is a comforting and hearty dish that's perfect for using up leftover turkey. It's packed with flavor and wholesome ingredients, making it a satisfying meal for any occasion!

Sweet Potato and Black Bean Enchilada Casserole

Ingredients:

- 2 large sweet potatoes, peeled and diced
- 1 tablespoon olive oil
- 1 onion, diced
- 2 cloves garlic, minced
- 1 bell pepper, diced
- 1 can (15 ounces) black beans, drained and rinsed
- 1 cup frozen corn kernels
- 1 can (15 ounces) enchilada sauce
- 1 teaspoon ground cumin
- 1 teaspoon chili powder
- Salt and pepper to taste
- 12 corn tortillas
- 2 cups shredded Mexican blend cheese
- Chopped fresh cilantro, for garnish (optional)
- Sour cream or Greek yogurt, for serving (optional)
- Sliced avocado, for serving (optional)

Instructions:

1. Preheat your oven to 375°F (190°C). Grease a 9x13-inch baking dish with cooking spray or olive oil.
2. Place the diced sweet potatoes in a microwave-safe bowl and microwave on high for 5-6 minutes, or until they are tender but not mushy.
3. In a large skillet, heat the olive oil over medium heat. Add the diced onion and cook until softened, about 3-4 minutes. Add the minced garlic and diced bell pepper, and cook for another 2-3 minutes until fragrant.
4. Add the cooked sweet potatoes, black beans, frozen corn kernels, enchilada sauce, ground cumin, chili powder, salt, and pepper to the skillet. Mix well to combine and cook for another 2-3 minutes until heated through.
5. Spread a thin layer of the sweet potato and black bean mixture on the bottom of the prepared baking dish.
6. Layer 4 corn tortillas on top of the sweet potato mixture, overlapping them slightly to cover the bottom of the dish.

7. Spread another layer of the sweet potato and black bean mixture over the tortillas.
8. Sprinkle 1/3 of the shredded cheese over the sweet potato mixture.
9. Repeat the layers: tortillas, sweet potato mixture, and shredded cheese, ending with a layer of shredded cheese on top.
10. Cover the baking dish with aluminum foil and bake in the preheated oven for 25 minutes.
11. Remove the foil and bake for an additional 10-15 minutes, or until the cheese is melted and bubbly.
12. Remove from the oven and let it cool for a few minutes before slicing.
13. Garnish with chopped fresh cilantro, if desired, and serve with sour cream or Greek yogurt and sliced avocado on the side.

This sweet potato and black bean enchilada casserole is a flavorful and satisfying dish that's perfect for a weeknight dinner or for entertaining guests. It's packed with wholesome ingredients and delicious Mexican flavors!

Sausage and Egg Breakfast Casserole

Ingredients:

- 1 pound breakfast sausage
- 6 large eggs
- 1 cup milk
- 1 teaspoon Dijon mustard
- Salt and pepper to taste
- 6 slices bread, cubed (day-old bread works well)
- 1 cup shredded cheddar cheese
- Optional toppings: chopped green onions, diced tomatoes, sliced mushrooms

Instructions:

1. Preheat your oven to 350°F (175°C). Grease a 9x13-inch baking dish with cooking spray or butter.
2. In a skillet over medium heat, cook the breakfast sausage until browned and cooked through, breaking it up into crumbles as it cooks. Drain any excess fat.
3. In a large mixing bowl, whisk together the eggs, milk, Dijon mustard, salt, and pepper until well combined.
4. Add the cubed bread to the egg mixture and toss to coat evenly. Let it sit for a few minutes to allow the bread to absorb the liquid.
5. Stir in the cooked sausage and shredded cheddar cheese until evenly distributed throughout the mixture.
6. Pour the mixture into the prepared baking dish and spread it out evenly.
7. Bake in the preheated oven for 35-40 minutes, or until the casserole is set and golden brown on top.
8. Remove from the oven and let it cool for a few minutes before slicing.
9. Garnish with chopped green onions, diced tomatoes, sliced mushrooms, or any other toppings of your choice.
10. Serve the sausage and egg breakfast casserole warm and enjoy!

This sausage and egg breakfast casserole is perfect for feeding a crowd or for meal prep. It's hearty, satisfying, and packed with protein to keep you full until lunchtime!

Mediterranean Eggplant Casserole

Ingredients:

- 2 large eggplants, sliced into rounds
- Salt
- Olive oil
- 1 onion, finely chopped
- 3 cloves garlic, minced
- 1 red bell pepper, diced
- 1 yellow bell pepper, diced
- 1 can (14 ounces) diced tomatoes
- 1/4 cup chopped fresh basil
- 1/4 cup chopped fresh parsley
- 1 teaspoon dried oregano
- 1/2 teaspoon dried thyme
- Salt and pepper to taste
- 1 cup crumbled feta cheese
- 1/4 cup grated Parmesan cheese
- Optional garnish: chopped fresh parsley or basil

Instructions:

1. Preheat your oven to 400°F (200°C). Grease a 9x13-inch baking dish with olive oil or cooking spray.
2. Place the eggplant slices in a colander and sprinkle them with salt. Let them sit for about 15-20 minutes to release excess moisture. Rinse the eggplant slices under cold water and pat them dry with paper towels.
3. Heat a drizzle of olive oil in a large skillet over medium heat. Add the chopped onion and cook until softened, about 3-4 minutes. Add the minced garlic and diced bell peppers, and cook for another 3-4 minutes until the peppers are tender.
4. Stir in the diced tomatoes, chopped basil, chopped parsley, dried oregano, and dried thyme. Season with salt and pepper to taste. Cook for 5-7 minutes, stirring occasionally, until the mixture thickens slightly.
5. Arrange half of the eggplant slices in the bottom of the prepared baking dish, overlapping them slightly.

6. Spoon half of the tomato and pepper mixture over the eggplant slices, spreading it out evenly.
7. Sprinkle half of the crumbled feta cheese over the tomato and pepper mixture.
8. Repeat the layers with the remaining eggplant slices, tomato and pepper mixture, and crumbled feta cheese.
9. Sprinkle the grated Parmesan cheese over the top of the casserole.
10. Cover the baking dish with aluminum foil and bake in the preheated oven for 25-30 minutes.
11. Remove the foil and bake for an additional 10-15 minutes, or until the cheese is melted and bubbly, and the eggplant is tender.
12. Remove from the oven and let it cool for a few minutes before serving.
13. Garnish with chopped fresh parsley or basil, if desired.

This Mediterranean eggplant casserole is a delicious and satisfying vegetarian dish that's perfect for a weeknight dinner or for entertaining guests. It's packed with flavor from the tomatoes, peppers, and herbs, and the creamy feta cheese adds a wonderful richness to the dish. Enjoy!

Chicken Alfredo Pasta Bake

Ingredients:

- 12 ounces pasta (such as penne or rotini)
- 2 cups cooked chicken, shredded or diced
- 2 cups Alfredo sauce (store-bought or homemade)
- 1 cup shredded mozzarella cheese
- 1/2 cup grated Parmesan cheese
- 1/4 cup chopped fresh parsley (optional, for garnish)
- Salt and pepper to taste

Instructions:

1. Preheat your oven to 375°F (190°C). Grease a 9x13-inch baking dish with cooking spray or butter.
2. Cook the pasta according to the package instructions until al dente. Drain the pasta and transfer it to a large mixing bowl.
3. Add the cooked chicken and Alfredo sauce to the bowl with the pasta. Season with salt and pepper to taste. Mix until the pasta and chicken are evenly coated with the sauce.
4. Transfer the pasta and chicken mixture to the prepared baking dish and spread it out evenly.
5. Sprinkle the shredded mozzarella cheese over the top of the pasta.
6. Sprinkle the grated Parmesan cheese over the mozzarella cheese.
7. Cover the baking dish with aluminum foil and bake in the preheated oven for 20-25 minutes, or until the cheese is melted and bubbly.
8. Remove the foil and bake for an additional 5-10 minutes, or until the cheese is golden brown on top.
9. Remove from the oven and let it cool for a few minutes before serving.
10. Garnish with chopped fresh parsley, if desired.

This chicken alfredo pasta bake is a comforting and satisfying dish that's perfect for a family dinner or potluck gathering. It's creamy, cheesy, and packed with flavor, making it a favorite among both kids and adults alike!

Cheesy Potato Casserole

Ingredients:

- 4 cups diced potatoes (about 4 medium potatoes)
- 1/2 cup sour cream
- 1/4 cup melted butter
- 1 can (10.75 ounces) condensed cream of chicken soup
- 2 cups shredded cheddar cheese, divided
- 1/4 cup chopped green onions (optional)
- Salt and pepper to taste
- 1 cup crushed cornflakes or breadcrumbs (for topping)
- 2 tablespoons melted butter (for topping)

Instructions:

1. Preheat your oven to 350°F (175°C). Grease a 9x13-inch baking dish with cooking spray or butter.
2. In a large mixing bowl, combine the diced potatoes, sour cream, melted butter, condensed cream of chicken soup, 1 cup of shredded cheddar cheese, chopped green onions (if using), salt, and pepper. Mix until well combined.
3. Spread the potato mixture evenly into the prepared baking dish.
4. In a small bowl, combine the crushed cornflakes or breadcrumbs with the melted butter. Mix until the crumbs are evenly coated.
5. Sprinkle the remaining 1 cup of shredded cheddar cheese over the top of the potato mixture in the baking dish.
6. Sprinkle the buttered cornflakes or breadcrumbs evenly over the cheese layer.
7. Cover the baking dish with aluminum foil and bake in the preheated oven for 30 minutes.
8. Remove the foil and bake for an additional 15-20 minutes, or until the cheese is melted and bubbly, and the potatoes are tender.
9. Remove from the oven and let it cool for a few minutes before serving.
10. Serve the cheesy potato casserole warm as a delicious side dish for any meal.

This cheesy potato casserole is a crowd-pleasing comfort food that's perfect for potlucks, holidays, or any occasion. It's creamy, cheesy, and irresistibly delicious!

Egg and Veggie Breakfast Casserole

Ingredients:

- 8 large eggs
- 1/2 cup milk
- Salt and pepper to taste
- 1 tablespoon olive oil
- 1 onion, diced
- 2 cloves garlic, minced
- 1 bell pepper, diced
- 1 zucchini, diced
- 1 cup sliced mushrooms
- 2 cups baby spinach
- 1 cup cherry tomatoes, halved
- 1 cup shredded cheddar cheese
- Optional add-ins: cooked sausage, bacon, or ham

Instructions:

1. Preheat your oven to 375°F (190°C). Grease a 9x13-inch baking dish with cooking spray or butter.
2. In a large mixing bowl, whisk together the eggs and milk until well combined. Season with salt and pepper to taste. Set aside.
3. In a large skillet, heat the olive oil over medium heat. Add the diced onion and cook until softened, about 3-4 minutes. Add the minced garlic and cook for another 1-2 minutes until fragrant.
4. Add the diced bell pepper, zucchini, and sliced mushrooms to the skillet. Cook for 5-6 minutes, or until the vegetables are tender.
5. Add the baby spinach and cherry tomatoes to the skillet. Cook for an additional 2-3 minutes, or until the spinach is wilted and the tomatoes are softened.
6. Transfer the cooked vegetables to the prepared baking dish, spreading them out evenly.
7. If using any optional add-ins such as cooked sausage, bacon, or ham, scatter them over the vegetables in the baking dish.
8. Pour the egg mixture over the vegetables and optional add-ins in the baking dish.
9. Sprinkle the shredded cheddar cheese evenly over the top of the egg mixture.

10. Bake in the preheated oven for 25-30 minutes, or until the eggs are set and the cheese is melted and golden brown on top.
11. Remove from the oven and let it cool for a few minutes before slicing.
12. Serve the egg and veggie breakfast casserole warm, garnished with chopped fresh herbs if desired.

This egg and veggie breakfast casserole is a nutritious and satisfying way to start your day. It's packed with protein, fiber, and vitamins from the eggs and colorful vegetables, making it a healthy and delicious option for breakfast or brunch!

Italian Sausage and Pasta Casserole

Ingredients:

- 8 ounces pasta (such as penne or rotini)
- 1 tablespoon olive oil
- 1 pound Italian sausage (mild or spicy), casings removed
- 1 onion, diced
- 2 cloves garlic, minced
- 1 bell pepper, diced
- 1 zucchini, diced
- 1 can (14.5 ounces) diced tomatoes, drained
- 1 can (8 ounces) tomato sauce
- 1 teaspoon dried oregano
- 1 teaspoon dried basil
- Salt and pepper to taste
- 1 cup shredded mozzarella cheese
- 1/4 cup grated Parmesan cheese
- Fresh basil leaves, chopped (for garnish, optional)

Instructions:

1. Preheat your oven to 375°F (190°C). Grease a 9x13-inch baking dish with cooking spray or olive oil.
2. Cook the pasta according to the package instructions until al dente. Drain and set aside.
3. In a large skillet, heat the olive oil over medium heat. Add the Italian sausage and cook until browned, breaking it up into crumbles as it cooks. Drain any excess fat.
4. Add the diced onion, minced garlic, diced bell pepper, and diced zucchini to the skillet with the cooked sausage. Cook for 5-7 minutes, or until the vegetables are softened.
5. Stir in the drained diced tomatoes, tomato sauce, dried oregano, and dried basil. Season with salt and pepper to taste. Cook for another 5 minutes, stirring occasionally.
6. In the prepared baking dish, combine the cooked pasta and sausage mixture, mixing until well combined.
7. Sprinkle the shredded mozzarella cheese evenly over the top of the pasta and sausage mixture.

8. Sprinkle the grated Parmesan cheese evenly over the mozzarella cheese.
9. Cover the baking dish with aluminum foil and bake in the preheated oven for 20 minutes.
10. Remove the foil and bake for an additional 10-15 minutes, or until the cheese is melted and bubbly, and the casserole is heated through.
11. Remove from the oven and let it cool for a few minutes before serving.
12. Garnish with chopped fresh basil leaves, if desired.

This Italian sausage and pasta casserole is a comforting and satisfying meal that's perfect for busy weeknights or for feeding a crowd. It's packed with flavor from the Italian sausage, tomatoes, and herbs, and the melted cheese on top adds a delicious finishing touch!

Vegan Lentil Shepherd's Pie

Ingredients:

For the lentil filling:

- 1 cup dry green or brown lentils, rinsed
- 3 cups vegetable broth
- 1 tablespoon olive oil
- 1 onion, diced
- 2 cloves garlic, minced
- 2 carrots, diced
- 2 stalks celery, diced
- 1 cup mushrooms, chopped
- 1 teaspoon dried thyme
- 1 teaspoon dried rosemary
- 1 teaspoon paprika
- Salt and pepper to taste
- 2 tablespoons tomato paste
- 2 tablespoons soy sauce or tamari
- 2 tablespoons all-purpose flour (or gluten-free flour)

For the mashed potato topping:

- 4 large potatoes, peeled and diced
- 1/4 cup vegan butter or olive oil
- 1/2 cup non-dairy milk (such as almond, soy, or oat milk)
- Salt and pepper to taste

Instructions:

1. Preheat your oven to 375°F (190°C). Grease a 9x13-inch baking dish with cooking spray or olive oil.
2. In a large pot, combine the lentils and vegetable broth. Bring to a boil, then reduce the heat to low and simmer for 20-25 minutes, or until the lentils are tender and the broth is absorbed. Drain any excess liquid and set aside.

3. In a large skillet, heat the olive oil over medium heat. Add the diced onion and cook until softened, about 3-4 minutes. Add the minced garlic and cook for another 1-2 minutes until fragrant.
4. Add the diced carrots, celery, and chopped mushrooms to the skillet. Cook for 5-6 minutes, or until the vegetables are tender.
5. Stir in the dried thyme, dried rosemary, paprika, salt, and pepper. Cook for another minute, then add the cooked lentils to the skillet.
6. Stir in the tomato paste and soy sauce (or tamari) until well combined. Sprinkle the flour over the lentil mixture and stir until thickened. If the mixture is too dry, you can add a splash of vegetable broth or water.
7. Transfer the lentil filling to the prepared baking dish and spread it out evenly.
8. To make the mashed potato topping, place the diced potatoes in a large pot and cover with water. Bring to a boil, then reduce the heat to medium-low and simmer for 10-15 minutes, or until the potatoes are tender.
9. Drain the cooked potatoes and return them to the pot. Add the vegan butter or olive oil and non-dairy milk to the pot with the potatoes. Mash until smooth and creamy. Season with salt and pepper to taste.
10. Spread the mashed potatoes over the lentil filling in the baking dish, smoothing it out with a spatula.
11. Bake in the preheated oven for 25-30 minutes, or until the shepherd's pie is heated through and the mashed potato topping is golden brown on top.
12. Remove from the oven and let it cool for a few minutes before serving.
13. Serve the vegan lentil shepherd's pie warm, garnished with chopped fresh parsley or thyme if desired.

This vegan lentil shepherd's pie is a hearty and comforting dish that's perfect for a cozy dinner. It's packed with protein and fiber from the lentils and vegetables, and the creamy mashed potato topping adds a delicious finishing touch!

Chicken Parmesan Casserole

Ingredients:

For the chicken:

- 4 boneless, skinless chicken breasts
- Salt and pepper to taste
- 1 cup all-purpose flour
- 2 eggs, beaten
- 1 cup breadcrumbs
- 1/2 cup grated Parmesan cheese
- 2 tablespoons olive oil

For the casserole:

- 2 cups marinara sauce
- 1 cup shredded mozzarella cheese
- 1/4 cup grated Parmesan cheese
- Fresh basil leaves, chopped (for garnish, optional)

Instructions:

1. Preheat your oven to 375°F (190°C). Grease a 9x13-inch baking dish with cooking spray or olive oil.
2. Season the chicken breasts with salt and pepper to taste.
3. Set up a breading station: Place the all-purpose flour in one shallow dish, the beaten eggs in another shallow dish, and the breadcrumbs mixed with grated Parmesan cheese in a third shallow dish.
4. Dredge each chicken breast in the flour, shaking off any excess. Dip the chicken in the beaten eggs, allowing any excess to drip off. Finally, coat the chicken in the breadcrumb mixture, pressing gently to adhere.
5. Heat the olive oil in a large skillet over medium-high heat. Add the breaded chicken breasts to the skillet and cook for 3-4 minutes per side, or until golden brown. They do not need to be cooked through at this point, as they will finish cooking in the oven. Remove the chicken from the skillet and set aside.
6. Spread half of the marinara sauce evenly over the bottom of the prepared baking dish.

7. Place the browned chicken breasts on top of the marinara sauce in the baking dish.
8. Spoon the remaining marinara sauce over the chicken breasts, covering them completely.
9. Sprinkle the shredded mozzarella cheese evenly over the top of the chicken breasts.
10. Sprinkle the grated Parmesan cheese evenly over the mozzarella cheese.
11. Cover the baking dish with aluminum foil and bake in the preheated oven for 25 minutes.
12. Remove the foil and bake for an additional 10-15 minutes, or until the cheese is melted and bubbly, and the chicken is cooked through.
13. Remove from the oven and let it cool for a few minutes before serving.
14. Garnish with chopped fresh basil leaves, if desired.

This chicken parmesan casserole is a comforting and satisfying meal that's perfect for a family dinner. It has all the flavors of classic chicken parmesan but is easier to make since it's baked in one dish. Enjoy!

Baked Macaroni and Cheese Casserole

Ingredients:

- 12 ounces elbow macaroni
- 1/4 cup unsalted butter
- 1/4 cup all-purpose flour
- 2 cups milk
- 2 cups shredded sharp cheddar cheese
- 1 cup shredded mozzarella cheese
- 1/2 cup grated Parmesan cheese
- 1/2 teaspoon salt, or to taste
- 1/4 teaspoon black pepper, or to taste
- 1/4 teaspoon paprika
- 1/4 teaspoon garlic powder
- 1/4 teaspoon onion powder
- Optional topping: breadcrumbs mixed with melted butter

Instructions:

1. Preheat your oven to 350°F (175°C). Grease a 9x13-inch baking dish with cooking spray or butter.
2. Cook the elbow macaroni according to the package instructions until al dente. Drain and set aside.
3. In a large saucepan, melt the butter over medium heat. Add the flour and whisk until smooth, cooking for about 1 minute.
4. Gradually whisk in the milk, stirring constantly, until the mixture is smooth and thickened, about 5-7 minutes.
5. Reduce the heat to low and add the shredded cheddar cheese, shredded mozzarella cheese, and grated Parmesan cheese. Stir until the cheese is melted and the sauce is smooth.
6. Season the cheese sauce with salt, pepper, paprika, garlic powder, and onion powder, adjusting to taste.
7. Add the cooked elbow macaroni to the cheese sauce, stirring until well combined and the macaroni is evenly coated.
8. Transfer the macaroni and cheese mixture to the prepared baking dish, spreading it out evenly.

9. If desired, sprinkle breadcrumbs mixed with melted butter over the top of the macaroni and cheese for a crunchy topping.
10. Bake in the preheated oven for 25-30 minutes, or until the macaroni and cheese is bubbly and golden brown on top.
11. Remove from the oven and let it cool for a few minutes before serving.
12. Serve the baked macaroni and cheese casserole warm as a comforting and delicious side dish.

This baked macaroni and cheese casserole is creamy, cheesy, and satisfying, making it a favorite among kids and adults alike. Enjoy it as a side dish or as a main course for a cozy dinner!

Hawaiian Pineapple Chicken Casserole

Ingredients:

- 2 cups cooked chicken, shredded or diced
- 2 cups cooked white rice
- 1 can (20 ounces) pineapple chunks, drained (reserve juice)
- 1 red bell pepper, diced
- 1 green bell pepper, diced
- 1 onion, diced
- 1 cup shredded mozzarella cheese
- 1 cup shredded cheddar cheese
- 1 cup barbecue sauce
- 1/4 cup soy sauce
- 2 tablespoons brown sugar
- 2 tablespoons pineapple juice (reserved from the canned pineapple)
- 1 tablespoon olive oil
- Salt and pepper to taste
- Optional garnish: chopped green onions or fresh cilantro

Instructions:

1. Preheat your oven to 375°F (190°C). Grease a 9x13-inch baking dish with cooking spray or butter.
2. In a large skillet, heat the olive oil over medium heat. Add the diced onion and bell peppers, and cook until softened, about 5-7 minutes.
3. In a small bowl, whisk together the barbecue sauce, soy sauce, brown sugar, and pineapple juice.
4. In a large mixing bowl, combine the cooked chicken, cooked rice, drained pineapple chunks, sautéed onion and bell peppers, and barbecue sauce mixture. Season with salt and pepper to taste. Mix until well combined.
5. Transfer the chicken and rice mixture to the prepared baking dish, spreading it out evenly.
6. Sprinkle the shredded mozzarella cheese and shredded cheddar cheese evenly over the top of the casserole.
7. Cover the baking dish with aluminum foil and bake in the preheated oven for 20 minutes.

8. Remove the foil and bake for an additional 10-15 minutes, or until the cheese is melted and bubbly, and the casserole is heated through.
9. Remove from the oven and let it cool for a few minutes before serving.
10. Garnish with chopped green onions or fresh cilantro, if desired.

This Hawaiian pineapple chicken casserole is a sweet and savory dish that's sure to be a hit with the whole family. It's packed with flavor from the barbecue sauce, pineapple, and bell peppers, and the melted cheese on top adds a delicious finishing touch! Enjoy!

Cauliflower and Broccoli Gratin

Ingredients:

- 1 head cauliflower, cut into florets
- 1 head broccoli, cut into florets
- 2 tablespoons unsalted butter
- 2 tablespoons all-purpose flour
- 2 cups whole milk
- 1 cup shredded cheddar cheese
- 1/4 cup grated Parmesan cheese
- 1/4 teaspoon nutmeg
- Salt and pepper to taste
- 1/2 cup breadcrumbs
- 2 tablespoons melted butter
- Optional: chopped fresh parsley for garnish

Instructions:

1. Preheat your oven to 375°F (190°C). Grease a 9x13-inch baking dish with cooking spray or butter.
2. Bring a large pot of salted water to a boil. Add the cauliflower and broccoli florets and cook for 3-4 minutes, or until slightly tender. Drain and set aside.
3. In a medium saucepan, melt the unsalted butter over medium heat. Add the flour and whisk until smooth, cooking for about 1 minute.
4. Gradually whisk in the whole milk, stirring constantly, until the mixture is smooth and thickened, about 5-7 minutes.
5. Stir in the shredded cheddar cheese and grated Parmesan cheese until melted and smooth. Season with nutmeg, salt, and pepper to taste.
6. Place the cooked cauliflower and broccoli florets in the prepared baking dish. Pour the cheese sauce over the top, making sure to coat the vegetables evenly.
7. In a small bowl, mix together the breadcrumbs and melted butter until well combined. Sprinkle the breadcrumb mixture evenly over the top of the gratin.
8. Bake in the preheated oven for 25-30 minutes, or until the gratin is bubbly and golden brown on top.
9. Remove from the oven and let it cool for a few minutes before serving.
10. Garnish with chopped fresh parsley, if desired.

This cauliflower and broccoli gratin is a delicious and comforting side dish that's perfect for any occasion. The creamy cheese sauce and crispy breadcrumb topping make it irresistible! Enjoy!

Beef and Potato Hash Brown Casserole

Ingredients:

- 1 pound ground beef
- 1 onion, diced
- 2 cloves garlic, minced
- 1 teaspoon dried thyme
- 1 teaspoon dried rosemary
- Salt and pepper to taste
- 4 cups frozen hash browns, thawed
- 1 can (10.5 ounces) condensed cream of mushroom soup
- 1 cup sour cream
- 1 cup shredded cheddar cheese
- 1/4 cup chopped fresh parsley (optional, for garnish)

Instructions:

1. Preheat your oven to 375°F (190°C). Grease a 9x13-inch baking dish with cooking spray or butter.
2. In a large skillet, cook the ground beef over medium heat until browned, breaking it up into crumbles as it cooks. Drain any excess fat.
3. Add the diced onion and minced garlic to the skillet with the cooked ground beef. Cook for 3-4 minutes, or until the onion is softened and translucent.
4. Stir in the dried thyme, dried rosemary, salt, and pepper. Cook for another minute until fragrant. Remove from heat.
5. In a large mixing bowl, combine the thawed hash browns, condensed cream of mushroom soup, sour cream, and shredded cheddar cheese. Mix until well combined.
6. Add the cooked ground beef mixture to the bowl with the hash brown mixture. Stir until evenly distributed.
7. Transfer the mixture to the prepared baking dish, spreading it out evenly.
8. Bake in the preheated oven for 25-30 minutes, or until the casserole is heated through and bubbly around the edges.
9. If desired, broil for an additional 1-2 minutes to brown the top of the casserole.
10. Remove from the oven and let it cool for a few minutes before serving.
11. Garnish with chopped fresh parsley, if desired.

This beef and potato hash brown casserole is a hearty and comforting dish that's perfect for a cozy dinner. It's packed with savory flavors and creamy textures that the whole family will love! Enjoy!

Chicken and Rice Casserole

Ingredients:

- 2 cups cooked chicken, shredded or diced
- 1 cup uncooked white rice
- 2 cups chicken broth
- 1 can (10.5 ounces) condensed cream of chicken soup
- 1 cup frozen mixed vegetables (such as peas, carrots, corn)
- 1/2 cup sour cream
- 1 cup shredded cheddar cheese
- 1/2 teaspoon garlic powder
- 1/2 teaspoon onion powder
- Salt and pepper to taste
- Optional topping: crushed crackers or breadcrumbs mixed with melted butter

Instructions:

1. Preheat your oven to 375°F (190°C). Grease a 9x13-inch baking dish with cooking spray or butter.
2. In a large mixing bowl, combine the cooked chicken, uncooked rice, chicken broth, condensed cream of chicken soup, frozen mixed vegetables, sour cream, shredded cheddar cheese, garlic powder, onion powder, salt, and pepper. Mix until well combined.
3. Transfer the mixture to the prepared baking dish, spreading it out evenly.
4. If using the optional topping, sprinkle the crushed crackers or breadcrumbs mixed with melted butter evenly over the top of the casserole.
5. Cover the baking dish with aluminum foil and bake in the preheated oven for 45-50 minutes, or until the rice is cooked and the casserole is heated through.
6. Remove the foil and bake for an additional 10-15 minutes, or until the top is golden brown and bubbly.
7. Remove from the oven and let it cool for a few minutes before serving.
8. Serve the chicken and rice casserole warm as a comforting and satisfying meal.

This chicken and rice casserole is a timeless dish that's perfect for a cozy dinner or for feeding a crowd. It's creamy, cheesy, and packed with flavor, making it a favorite among both kids and adults alike! Enjoy!

Sausage and Spinach Breakfast Casserole

Ingredients:

- 1 pound breakfast sausage (pork or turkey), casings removed
- 1 onion, diced
- 2 cloves garlic, minced
- 6 cups baby spinach leaves
- 8 large eggs
- 1 cup milk
- 1 teaspoon dried thyme
- 1 teaspoon dried oregano
- Salt and pepper to taste
- 2 cups shredded cheddar cheese
- Optional: chopped fresh parsley for garnish

Instructions:

1. Preheat your oven to 375°F (190°C). Grease a 9x13-inch baking dish with cooking spray or butter.
2. In a large skillet, cook the breakfast sausage over medium heat until browned, breaking it up into crumbles as it cooks. Drain any excess fat.
3. Add the diced onion to the skillet with the cooked sausage and cook until softened, about 3-4 minutes.
4. Add the minced garlic to the skillet and cook for another 1-2 minutes until fragrant.
5. Add the baby spinach leaves to the skillet and cook until wilted, stirring occasionally. Remove from heat.
6. In a large mixing bowl, whisk together the eggs, milk, dried thyme, dried oregano, salt, and pepper until well combined.
7. Stir in the cooked sausage, onion, garlic, and spinach mixture into the egg mixture until evenly distributed.
8. Fold in 1 1/2 cups of shredded cheddar cheese into the egg mixture.
9. Pour the egg mixture into the prepared baking dish, spreading it out evenly.
10. Sprinkle the remaining 1/2 cup of shredded cheddar cheese evenly over the top of the casserole.

11. Bake in the preheated oven for 25-30 minutes, or until the casserole is set and the top is golden brown.
12. Remove from the oven and let it cool for a few minutes before serving.
13. Garnish with chopped fresh parsley, if desired.

This sausage and spinach breakfast casserole is a hearty and nutritious dish that's perfect for a weekend brunch or a special breakfast treat. It's packed with protein, vitamins, and flavor, making it a favorite among both kids and adults alike! Enjoy!

Vegetable Lasagna Casserole

Ingredients:

- 9 lasagna noodles
- 2 tablespoons olive oil
- 1 onion, diced
- 2 cloves garlic, minced
- 1 zucchini, diced
- 1 yellow squash, diced
- 1 bell pepper, diced
- 1 cup sliced mushrooms
- 1 cup spinach leaves
- 1 jar (24 ounces) marinara sauce
- 1 cup ricotta cheese
- 1 cup shredded mozzarella cheese
- 1/4 cup grated Parmesan cheese
- 1 teaspoon dried basil
- 1 teaspoon dried oregano
- Salt and pepper to taste
- Optional: chopped fresh parsley for garnish

Instructions:

1. Preheat your oven to 375°F (190°C). Grease a 9x13-inch baking dish with cooking spray or olive oil.
2. Cook the lasagna noodles according to the package instructions until al dente. Drain and set aside.
3. In a large skillet, heat the olive oil over medium heat. Add the diced onion and minced garlic, and cook until softened and fragrant, about 3-4 minutes.
4. Add the diced zucchini, yellow squash, bell pepper, mushrooms, and spinach leaves to the skillet. Cook until the vegetables are tender, about 5-7 minutes. Season with salt and pepper to taste.
5. Stir in the marinara sauce, dried basil, and dried oregano. Cook for another 2-3 minutes, then remove from heat.
6. In a small bowl, mix together the ricotta cheese, shredded mozzarella cheese, and grated Parmesan cheese.

7. Spread a thin layer of the vegetable sauce mixture on the bottom of the prepared baking dish.
8. Place 3 lasagna noodles on top of the sauce layer. Spread half of the ricotta cheese mixture over the noodles.
9. Spoon half of the vegetable sauce mixture over the ricotta cheese layer.
10. Repeat the layers with the remaining lasagna noodles, ricotta cheese mixture, and vegetable sauce mixture.
11. Cover the baking dish with aluminum foil and bake in the preheated oven for 30 minutes.
12. Remove the foil and bake for an additional 15-20 minutes, or until the lasagna noodles are tender and the cheese is melted and bubbly.
13. Remove from the oven and let it cool for a few minutes before serving.
14. Garnish with chopped fresh parsley, if desired.

This vegetable lasagna casserole is a nutritious and flavorful dish that's perfect for a vegetarian meal or for anyone looking to incorporate more vegetables into their diet. It's hearty, comforting, and packed with delicious flavors! Enjoy!

Tex-Mex Beef Enchilada Casserole

Ingredients:

- 1 pound ground beef
- 1 onion, diced
- 2 cloves garlic, minced
- 1 can (15 ounces) black beans, drained and rinsed
- 1 can (15 ounces) corn kernels, drained
- 1 can (10 ounces) diced tomatoes with green chilies, drained
- 1 can (10 ounces) red enchilada sauce
- 1 teaspoon ground cumin
- 1 teaspoon chili powder
- Salt and pepper to taste
- 10-12 corn tortillas
- 2 cups shredded Mexican cheese blend
- Optional toppings: sliced jalapeños, diced avocado, chopped cilantro, sour cream, salsa

Instructions:

1. Preheat your oven to 375°F (190°C). Grease a 9x13-inch baking dish with cooking spray or olive oil.
2. In a large skillet, cook the ground beef over medium heat until browned, breaking it up into crumbles as it cooks. Drain any excess fat.
3. Add the diced onion and minced garlic to the skillet with the cooked beef. Cook until the onion is softened, about 3-4 minutes.
4. Stir in the black beans, corn kernels, diced tomatoes with green chilies, red enchilada sauce, ground cumin, chili powder, salt, and pepper. Cook for another 3-4 minutes, stirring occasionally, until heated through.
5. Spread a thin layer of the beef and bean mixture on the bottom of the prepared baking dish.
6. Layer half of the corn tortillas on top of the beef mixture, tearing them if needed to fit the pan.
7. Spread half of the remaining beef and bean mixture over the tortillas.
8. Sprinkle half of the shredded Mexican cheese blend evenly over the beef mixture.

9. Repeat the layers with the remaining tortillas, beef and bean mixture, and shredded cheese.
10. Cover the baking dish with aluminum foil and bake in the preheated oven for 25-30 minutes.
11. Remove the foil and bake for an additional 10-15 minutes, or until the cheese is melted and bubbly and the edges are golden brown.
12. Remove from the oven and let it cool for a few minutes before serving.
13. Serve the Tex-Mex beef enchilada casserole warm, topped with optional toppings such as sliced jalapeños, diced avocado, chopped cilantro, sour cream, and salsa.

This Tex-Mex beef enchilada casserole is a flavorful and satisfying dish that's perfect for a weeknight dinner or for feeding a crowd. It's packed with protein, fiber, and delicious Tex-Mex flavors that everyone will love! Enjoy!

Greek Moussaka Casserole

Ingredients:

For the eggplant layer:

- 2 large eggplants, sliced into 1/4-inch rounds
- Salt
- Olive oil for brushing

For the meat sauce:

- 1 tablespoon olive oil
- 1 onion, finely chopped
- 3 cloves garlic, minced
- 1 pound ground lamb or beef
- 1 can (14 ounces) crushed tomatoes
- 2 tablespoons tomato paste
- 1 teaspoon dried oregano
- 1/2 teaspoon ground cinnamon
- Salt and pepper to taste

For the béchamel sauce:

- 4 tablespoons unsalted butter
- 1/4 cup all-purpose flour
- 2 cups milk
- Salt and pepper to taste
- 1/4 teaspoon ground nutmeg
- 2 large eggs
- 1/2 cup grated Parmesan cheese

Instructions:

1. Preheat your oven to 400°F (200°C). Grease a 9x13-inch baking dish with olive oil.
2. Place the eggplant slices on a baking sheet lined with parchment paper. Sprinkle both sides of the eggplant slices with salt and let them sit for about 30 minutes to draw out excess moisture.
3. Pat the eggplant slices dry with paper towels. Brush both sides of the eggplant slices with olive oil. Arrange the slices on the baking sheet in a single layer. Bake in the preheated oven for 15-20 minutes, or until the eggplant is tender and lightly browned. Remove from the oven and set aside.
4. To make the meat sauce, heat olive oil in a large skillet over medium heat. Add the chopped onion and minced garlic, and cook until softened and fragrant, about 3-4 minutes.
5. Add the ground lamb or beef to the skillet and cook until browned, breaking it up with a spoon as it cooks.
6. Stir in the crushed tomatoes, tomato paste, dried oregano, ground cinnamon, salt, and pepper. Simmer for about 15-20 minutes, stirring occasionally, until the sauce thickens. Remove from heat and set aside.
7. To make the béchamel sauce, melt the butter in a saucepan over medium heat. Whisk in the flour and cook for 1-2 minutes, stirring constantly, until golden brown.
8. Gradually whisk in the milk, stirring constantly, until the mixture is smooth and thickened. Season with salt, pepper, and ground nutmeg.
9. In a separate bowl, beat the eggs. Gradually whisk the beaten eggs into the béchamel sauce until well combined.
10. Stir in the grated Parmesan cheese until melted and smooth. Remove from heat and set aside.
11. To assemble the moussaka casserole, spread half of the meat sauce in the bottom of the prepared baking dish.
12. Arrange half of the baked eggplant slices over the meat sauce in the baking dish.
13. Spread the remaining meat sauce over the eggplant slices.
14. Arrange the remaining baked eggplant slices over the meat sauce.
15. Pour the béchamel sauce over the top of the casserole, spreading it out evenly with a spatula.
16. Bake in the preheated oven for 45-50 minutes, or until the top is golden brown and bubbly.
17. Remove from the oven and let it cool for a few minutes before serving.
18. Serve the moussaka casserole warm, sliced into squares. Enjoy!

This Greek moussaka casserole is a flavorful and comforting dish that's perfect for a special occasion or a hearty family dinner. It's packed with layers of eggplant, meat sauce, and creamy béchamel sauce, creating a delicious and satisfying meal that everyone will love!

Breakfast Burrito Casserole

Ingredients:

- 6 large eggs
- 1/4 cup milk
- Salt and pepper to taste
- 1 pound breakfast sausage
- 1 onion, diced
- 1 bell pepper, diced
- 1 jalapeño, diced (optional)
- 1 cup diced tomatoes
- 1 cup shredded cheddar cheese
- 1 cup shredded Monterey Jack cheese
- 6 large flour tortillas
- Salsa, sour cream, avocado slices, chopped cilantro (optional, for serving)

Instructions:

1. Preheat your oven to 375°F (190°C). Grease a 9x13-inch baking dish with cooking spray or butter.
2. In a large mixing bowl, whisk together the eggs, milk, salt, and pepper until well combined. Set aside.
3. In a large skillet, cook the breakfast sausage over medium heat until browned and cooked through, breaking it up into crumbles as it cooks. Remove from the skillet and drain any excess fat.
4. In the same skillet, add the diced onion, bell pepper, and jalapeño (if using). Cook until the vegetables are softened, about 5-7 minutes.
5. Return the cooked sausage to the skillet with the vegetables. Add the diced tomatoes and stir until heated through. Remove from heat.
6. Spread a thin layer of the sausage and vegetable mixture on the bottom of the prepared baking dish.
7. Place a layer of flour tortillas on top of the sausage mixture, overlapping them slightly to cover the bottom of the dish.
8. Pour half of the beaten egg mixture over the tortillas, spreading it out evenly.
9. Sprinkle half of the shredded cheddar cheese and half of the shredded Monterey Jack cheese over the egg mixture.

10. Repeat the layers with the remaining sausage and vegetable mixture, flour tortillas, beaten egg mixture, and shredded cheeses.
11. Cover the baking dish with aluminum foil and bake in the preheated oven for 30 minutes.
12. Remove the foil and bake for an additional 10-15 minutes, or until the eggs are set and the cheese is melted and bubbly.
13. Remove from the oven and let it cool for a few minutes before serving.
14. Serve the breakfast burrito casserole warm, sliced into squares. Serve with salsa, sour cream, avocado slices, and chopped cilantro if desired.

This breakfast burrito casserole is a hearty and satisfying meal that's perfect for feeding a crowd or for meal prep. It's packed with savory flavors and customizable toppings, making it a family favorite for breakfast or brunch! Enjoy!

Creamy Spinach and Mushroom Pasta Bake

Ingredients:

- 12 ounces (340g) penne pasta
- 2 tablespoons olive oil
- 8 ounces (225g) mushrooms, sliced
- 3 cloves garlic, minced
- 4 cups fresh spinach leaves
- 2 tablespoons butter
- 2 tablespoons all-purpose flour
- 2 cups milk (whole or 2% recommended)
- 1 cup grated Parmesan cheese
- Salt and pepper to taste
- 1/2 teaspoon dried thyme
- 1/2 teaspoon dried oregano
- 1/4 teaspoon red pepper flakes (optional)
- 1 cup shredded mozzarella cheese
- Fresh parsley, chopped, for garnish (optional)

Instructions:

1. Preheat your oven to 375°F (190°C). Grease a 9x13-inch baking dish with cooking spray or butter.
2. Cook the penne pasta according to the package instructions until al dente. Drain and set aside.
3. In a large skillet, heat the olive oil over medium heat. Add the sliced mushrooms and cook until they release their moisture and turn golden brown, about 5-7 minutes.
4. Add the minced garlic to the skillet and cook for another 1-2 minutes until fragrant.
5. Add the fresh spinach leaves to the skillet and cook until wilted, stirring occasionally. Remove from heat and set aside.
6. In a separate saucepan, melt the butter over medium heat. Whisk in the all-purpose flour and cook for 1-2 minutes to make a roux.
7. Gradually whisk in the milk, stirring constantly, until the mixture is smooth and thickened.

8. Stir in the grated Parmesan cheese until melted and the sauce is creamy. Season with salt, pepper, dried thyme, dried oregano, and red pepper flakes (if using).
9. In a large mixing bowl, combine the cooked penne pasta, mushroom-spinach mixture, and creamy Parmesan sauce. Mix until well coated.
10. Transfer the pasta mixture to the prepared baking dish, spreading it out evenly.
11. Sprinkle the shredded mozzarella cheese evenly over the top of the pasta.
12. Cover the baking dish with aluminum foil and bake in the preheated oven for 20 minutes.
13. Remove the foil and bake for an additional 10-15 minutes, or until the cheese is melted and bubbly and the edges are golden brown.
14. Remove from the oven and let it cool for a few minutes before serving.
15. Garnish with chopped fresh parsley, if desired.

This creamy spinach and mushroom pasta bake is a comforting and satisfying dish that's perfect for a cozy dinner or for entertaining guests. It's packed with savory flavors and creamy textures that the whole family will love! Enjoy!

Mexican Chicken Tortilla Casserole

Ingredients:

- 2 cups cooked chicken, shredded or diced
- 1 onion, diced
- 1 bell pepper, diced
- 1 can (15 ounces) black beans, drained and rinsed
- 1 can (15 ounces) corn kernels, drained
- 1 can (10 ounces) diced tomatoes with green chilies, drained
- 1 teaspoon chili powder
- 1 teaspoon ground cumin
- 1/2 teaspoon garlic powder
- Salt and pepper to taste
- 10-12 corn tortillas
- 2 cups shredded Mexican cheese blend
- Optional toppings: diced avocado, chopped cilantro, sour cream, salsa

Instructions:

1. Preheat your oven to 375°F (190°C). Grease a 9x13-inch baking dish with cooking spray or olive oil.
2. In a large mixing bowl, combine the cooked chicken, diced onion, diced bell pepper, black beans, corn kernels, diced tomatoes with green chilies, chili powder, ground cumin, garlic powder, salt, and pepper. Mix until well combined.
3. Cut the corn tortillas into quarters.
4. Arrange a layer of corn tortilla quarters on the bottom of the prepared baking dish, overlapping them slightly to cover the bottom.
5. Spread a layer of the chicken and vegetable mixture over the tortillas.
6. Sprinkle a layer of shredded Mexican cheese blend over the chicken mixture.
7. Repeat the layers with the remaining corn tortillas, chicken and vegetable mixture, and shredded cheese.
8. Cover the baking dish with aluminum foil and bake in the preheated oven for 25 minutes.
9. Remove the foil and bake for an additional 10-15 minutes, or until the cheese is melted and bubbly and the edges are golden brown.
10. Remove from the oven and let it cool for a few minutes before serving.

11. Serve the Mexican chicken tortilla casserole warm, topped with optional toppings such as diced avocado, chopped cilantro, sour cream, and salsa.

This Mexican chicken tortilla casserole is a flavorful and satisfying dish that's perfect for a weeknight dinner or for entertaining guests. It's packed with protein, fiber, and delicious Mexican flavors that everyone will love! Enjoy!

Butternut Squash and Kale Quinoa Casserole

Ingredients:

- 1 cup quinoa, rinsed
- 2 cups vegetable broth or water
- 1 small butternut squash, peeled, seeded, and diced
- 1 tablespoon olive oil
- 1 onion, diced
- 2 cloves garlic, minced
- 4 cups chopped kale leaves, stems removed
- 1 teaspoon dried thyme
- 1/2 teaspoon dried sage
- Salt and pepper to taste
- 1/2 cup grated Parmesan cheese (optional)
- 1/4 cup chopped fresh parsley (optional)

Instructions:

1. Preheat your oven to 375°F (190°C). Grease a 9x13-inch baking dish with cooking spray or olive oil.
2. In a medium saucepan, combine the quinoa and vegetable broth or water. Bring to a boil, then reduce the heat to low, cover, and simmer for 15-20 minutes, or until the quinoa is cooked and the liquid is absorbed. Remove from heat and set aside.
3. While the quinoa is cooking, heat the olive oil in a large skillet over medium heat. Add the diced butternut squash and cook for 5-7 minutes, or until slightly softened.
4. Add the diced onion to the skillet with the butternut squash and cook for another 3-4 minutes, or until the onion is softened and translucent.
5. Add the minced garlic, chopped kale leaves, dried thyme, dried sage, salt, and pepper to the skillet. Cook for 3-4 minutes, stirring occasionally, until the kale is wilted and tender.
6. In a large mixing bowl, combine the cooked quinoa and the cooked butternut squash and kale mixture. Stir until well combined.
7. Transfer the quinoa mixture to the prepared baking dish, spreading it out evenly.
8. If desired, sprinkle the grated Parmesan cheese evenly over the top of the casserole.

9. Cover the baking dish with aluminum foil and bake in the preheated oven for 20 minutes.
10. Remove the foil and bake for an additional 10-15 minutes, or until the casserole is heated through and the edges are golden brown.
11. Remove from the oven and let it cool for a few minutes before serving.
12. Garnish with chopped fresh parsley, if desired.

This butternut squash and kale quinoa casserole is a nutritious and flavorful dish that's perfect for a cozy dinner or for entertaining guests. It's packed with wholesome ingredients and delicious flavors that everyone will love! Enjoy!

Baked Spaghetti Squash Casserole

Ingredients:

- 1 medium spaghetti squash
- 1 tablespoon olive oil
- 1 onion, diced
- 2 cloves garlic, minced
- 1 bell pepper, diced
- 1 pound ground turkey or beef
- 1 can (14.5 ounces) diced tomatoes, drained
- 1 can (8 ounces) tomato sauce
- 1 teaspoon dried oregano
- 1 teaspoon dried basil
- Salt and pepper to taste
- 1 cup shredded mozzarella cheese
- 1/4 cup grated Parmesan cheese
- Fresh basil leaves, chopped (optional, for garnish)

Instructions:

1. Preheat your oven to 375°F (190°C). Grease a 9x13-inch baking dish with cooking spray or olive oil.
2. Cut the spaghetti squash in half lengthwise and scoop out the seeds. Place the squash halves cut side down on a baking sheet lined with parchment paper. Bake in the preheated oven for 40-50 minutes, or until the squash is tender and easily pierced with a fork. Remove from the oven and let it cool slightly.
3. While the spaghetti squash is baking, heat the olive oil in a large skillet over medium heat. Add the diced onion and minced garlic, and cook until softened and fragrant, about 3-4 minutes.
4. Add the diced bell pepper to the skillet and cook for another 2-3 minutes.
5. Add the ground turkey or beef to the skillet and cook until browned, breaking it up into crumbles as it cooks.
6. Stir in the diced tomatoes, tomato sauce, dried oregano, dried basil, salt, and pepper. Simmer for about 10 minutes, stirring occasionally, to allow the flavors to meld. Remove from heat and set aside.

7. Once the spaghetti squash is cool enough to handle, use a fork to scrape the flesh into spaghetti-like strands. Place the spaghetti squash strands in a large mixing bowl.
8. Add the cooked meat and tomato sauce mixture to the bowl with the spaghetti squash. Mix until well combined.
9. Transfer the spaghetti squash mixture to the prepared baking dish, spreading it out evenly.
10. Sprinkle the shredded mozzarella cheese and grated Parmesan cheese evenly over the top of the casserole.
11. Cover the baking dish with aluminum foil and bake in the preheated oven for 20 minutes.
12. Remove the foil and bake for an additional 10-15 minutes, or until the cheese is melted and bubbly and the edges are golden brown.
13. Remove from the oven and let it cool for a few minutes before serving.
14. Garnish with chopped fresh basil leaves, if desired.

This baked spaghetti squash casserole is a healthier alternative to traditional pasta dishes, and it's packed with flavor and nutritious ingredients. It's a satisfying meal that's perfect for a cozy dinner or for feeding a crowd! Enjoy!

Buffalo Chicken Pasta Bake

Ingredients:

- 12 ounces (340g) penne pasta
- 2 cups cooked and shredded chicken (rotisserie chicken works well)
- 1 cup buffalo sauce
- 1/2 cup ranch dressing
- 1 cup shredded mozzarella cheese
- 1 cup shredded cheddar cheese
- 1/4 cup blue cheese crumbles (optional)
- 2 green onions, thinly sliced
- Salt and pepper to taste
- Cooking spray

Instructions:

1. Preheat your oven to 375°F (190°C). Grease a 9x13-inch baking dish with cooking spray.
2. Cook the penne pasta according to the package instructions until al dente. Drain and set aside.
3. In a large mixing bowl, combine the shredded chicken, buffalo sauce, ranch dressing, shredded mozzarella cheese, shredded cheddar cheese, and blue cheese crumbles (if using). Mix until well combined.
4. Add the cooked penne pasta to the bowl with the chicken mixture. Season with salt and pepper to taste. Mix until the pasta is evenly coated with the sauce.
5. Transfer the buffalo chicken pasta mixture to the prepared baking dish, spreading it out evenly.
6. Bake in the preheated oven for 20-25 minutes, or until the cheese is melted and bubbly and the edges are golden brown.
7. Remove from the oven and let it cool for a few minutes before serving.
8. Garnish with sliced green onions before serving.

This buffalo chicken pasta bake is a delicious and satisfying dish that's perfect for game day gatherings, potlucks, or weeknight dinners. It's packed with spicy buffalo flavor and creamy ranch dressing, and it's sure to be a hit with everyone! Enjoy!

Broccoli and Cheese Quiche Casserole

Ingredients:

- 1 unbaked pie crust (store-bought or homemade)
- 1 tablespoon olive oil
- 1 small onion, diced
- 2 cloves garlic, minced
- 2 cups fresh broccoli florets, chopped
- 4 large eggs
- 1 cup milk or half-and-half
- 1 cup shredded cheddar cheese
- 1/2 cup grated Parmesan cheese
- Salt and pepper to taste
- Pinch of nutmeg (optional)

Instructions:

1. Preheat your oven to 375°F (190°C). Grease a 9x13-inch baking dish with cooking spray.
2. Heat the olive oil in a skillet over medium heat. Add the diced onion and minced garlic, and cook until softened and fragrant, about 3-4 minutes.
3. Add the chopped broccoli florets to the skillet and cook for another 3-4 minutes, or until the broccoli is slightly tender. Remove from heat and let it cool slightly.
4. Roll out the pie crust and press it into the bottom and up the sides of the prepared baking dish.
5. In a mixing bowl, whisk together the eggs and milk until well combined. Season with salt, pepper, and a pinch of nutmeg (if using).
6. Sprinkle half of the shredded cheddar cheese and half of the grated Parmesan cheese over the bottom of the pie crust.
7. Spread the cooked broccoli mixture evenly over the cheese in the pie crust.
8. Pour the egg mixture over the broccoli in the pie crust, making sure it's evenly distributed.
9. Sprinkle the remaining shredded cheddar cheese and grated Parmesan cheese over the top of the quiche.
10. Bake in the preheated oven for 30-35 minutes, or until the quiche is set and the crust is golden brown.

11. Remove from the oven and let it cool for a few minutes before slicing and serving.
12. Serve the broccoli and cheese quiche casserole warm or at room temperature.

This broccoli and cheese quiche casserole is a delicious and comforting dish that's perfect for breakfast, brunch, or even dinner. It's packed with savory flavors and wholesome ingredients, making it a family favorite! Enjoy!

Italian Meatball Casserole

Ingredients:

For the meatballs:

- 1 pound ground beef
- 1/2 cup breadcrumbs
- 1/4 cup grated Parmesan cheese
- 1 egg
- 2 cloves garlic, minced
- 1 teaspoon dried oregano
- 1 teaspoon dried basil
- Salt and pepper to taste

For the casserole:

- 1 tablespoon olive oil
- 1 onion, diced
- 2 cloves garlic, minced
- 1 bell pepper, diced
- 1 can (14.5 ounces) diced tomatoes
- 1 can (8 ounces) tomato sauce
- 1 teaspoon dried oregano
- 1 teaspoon dried basil
- Salt and pepper to taste
- 1 cup shredded mozzarella cheese
- Fresh parsley, chopped (optional, for garnish)

Instructions:

1. Preheat your oven to 375°F (190°C). Grease a 9x13-inch baking dish with cooking spray or olive oil.
2. In a large mixing bowl, combine the ground beef, breadcrumbs, grated Parmesan cheese, egg, minced garlic, dried oregano, dried basil, salt, and pepper. Mix until well combined.
3. Shape the mixture into meatballs, about 1 inch in diameter. Place the meatballs in the prepared baking dish.

4. In a large skillet, heat the olive oil over medium heat. Add the diced onion and cook until softened, about 3-4 minutes. Add the minced garlic and diced bell pepper, and cook for another 2-3 minutes.
5. Add the diced tomatoes, tomato sauce, dried oregano, dried basil, salt, and pepper to the skillet. Stir until well combined. Simmer for about 5-7 minutes, stirring occasionally.
6. Pour the tomato sauce mixture over the meatballs in the baking dish, making sure the meatballs are covered with the sauce.
7. Cover the baking dish with aluminum foil and bake in the preheated oven for 25-30 minutes.
8. Remove the foil and sprinkle the shredded mozzarella cheese evenly over the top of the casserole.
9. Return the casserole to the oven and bake, uncovered, for an additional 10-15 minutes, or until the cheese is melted and bubbly and the meatballs are cooked through.
10. Remove from the oven and let it cool for a few minutes before serving.
11. Garnish with chopped fresh parsley, if desired.

This Italian meatball casserole is a flavorful and satisfying dish that's perfect for a cozy family dinner or for entertaining guests. It's packed with savory meatballs, tangy tomato sauce, and gooey melted cheese, creating a delicious and comforting meal that everyone will love! Enjoy!

Vegetarian Chili Cornbread Casserole

Ingredients:

For the vegetarian chili:

- 1 tablespoon olive oil
- 1 onion, diced
- 2 cloves garlic, minced
- 1 bell pepper, diced
- 1 jalapeño, diced (optional)
- 1 can (14.5 ounces) diced tomatoes
- 1 can (15 ounces) black beans, drained and rinsed
- 1 can (15 ounces) kidney beans, drained and rinsed
- 1 cup corn kernels (fresh, canned, or frozen)
- 1 cup vegetable broth
- 2 teaspoons chili powder
- 1 teaspoon ground cumin
- 1/2 teaspoon smoked paprika
- Salt and pepper to taste

For the cornbread topping:

- 1 cup yellow cornmeal
- 1 cup all-purpose flour
- 1 tablespoon baking powder
- 1/2 teaspoon salt
- 1 cup milk (dairy or plant-based)
- 1/4 cup melted butter or olive oil
- 1 egg
- 1 cup shredded cheddar cheese (optional)

Instructions:

1. Preheat your oven to 375°F (190°C). Grease a 9x13-inch baking dish with cooking spray or olive oil.

2. To make the vegetarian chili, heat the olive oil in a large skillet over medium heat. Add the diced onion and cook until softened, about 3-4 minutes. Add the minced garlic, diced bell pepper, and diced jalapeño (if using), and cook for another 2-3 minutes.
3. Stir in the diced tomatoes, black beans, kidney beans, corn kernels, vegetable broth, chili powder, ground cumin, smoked paprika, salt, and pepper. Bring to a simmer and cook for about 10-15 minutes, stirring occasionally, until the chili has thickened slightly.
4. While the chili is simmering, prepare the cornbread topping. In a mixing bowl, combine the yellow cornmeal, all-purpose flour, baking powder, and salt. In a separate bowl, whisk together the milk, melted butter or olive oil, and egg. Pour the wet ingredients into the dry ingredients and stir until just combined.
5. Pour the vegetarian chili into the prepared baking dish, spreading it out evenly.
6. If using, sprinkle the shredded cheddar cheese evenly over the top of the chili.
7. Carefully spread the cornbread batter over the top of the chili, covering it completely.
8. Bake in the preheated oven for 25-30 minutes, or until the cornbread is golden brown and cooked through.
9. Remove from the oven and let it cool for a few minutes before serving.
10. Serve the vegetarian chili cornbread casserole warm, topped with optional toppings such as sliced green onions, chopped cilantro, sour cream, or salsa.

This vegetarian chili cornbread casserole is a hearty and comforting meal that's perfect for a cozy dinner or for entertaining guests. It's packed with flavorful chili and topped with tender, golden cornbread, creating a delicious and satisfying dish that everyone will love! Enjoy!

Chicken and Stuffing Casserole

Ingredients:

- 4 cups cooked chicken, shredded or diced
- 1 can (10.5 ounces) condensed cream of chicken soup
- 1 cup sour cream
- 1 cup chicken broth
- 1 package (6 ounces) stuffing mix
- 1/2 cup (1 stick) unsalted butter, melted
- 1 cup frozen mixed vegetables (peas, carrots, corn)
- Salt and pepper to taste
- Chopped parsley for garnish (optional)

Instructions:

1. Preheat your oven to 375°F (190°C). Grease a 9x13-inch baking dish with cooking spray or butter.
2. In a large mixing bowl, combine the cooked chicken, condensed cream of chicken soup, sour cream, and chicken broth. Season with salt and pepper to taste. Mix until well combined.
3. Spread the chicken mixture evenly in the bottom of the prepared baking dish.
4. In a separate mixing bowl, combine the stuffing mix and melted butter. Stir until the stuffing mix is evenly coated with the butter.
5. Sprinkle the frozen mixed vegetables over the chicken mixture in the baking dish.
6. Spread the stuffing mixture evenly over the top of the vegetables and chicken mixture.
7. Cover the baking dish with aluminum foil and bake in the preheated oven for 25 minutes.
8. Remove the foil and bake for an additional 10-15 minutes, or until the stuffing is golden brown and crispy.
9. Remove from the oven and let it cool for a few minutes before serving.
10. Garnish with chopped parsley, if desired.

This chicken and stuffing casserole is a comforting and satisfying dish that's perfect for a cozy family dinner or for entertaining guests. It's packed with tender chicken, creamy sauce, flavorful stuffing, and wholesome vegetables, creating a delicious and hearty meal that everyone will love! Enjoy!

Ratatouille Casserole

Ingredients:

- 1 large eggplant, diced
- 2 medium zucchini, diced
- 2 bell peppers (red, yellow, or orange), diced
- 1 large onion, diced
- 4 cloves garlic, minced
- 2 cups cherry tomatoes, halved
- 1/4 cup tomato paste
- 2 tablespoons olive oil
- 1 teaspoon dried thyme
- 1 teaspoon dried oregano
- Salt and pepper to taste
- 1/4 cup chopped fresh basil
- 1/4 cup grated Parmesan cheese (optional)

Instructions:

1. Preheat your oven to 375°F (190°C). Grease a 9x13-inch baking dish with cooking spray or olive oil.
2. In a large skillet, heat the olive oil over medium heat. Add the diced onion and cook until softened, about 3-4 minutes. Add the minced garlic and cook for another 1-2 minutes, until fragrant.
3. Add the diced eggplant, zucchini, and bell peppers to the skillet. Cook, stirring occasionally, for about 5-7 minutes, until the vegetables start to soften.
4. Stir in the cherry tomatoes, tomato paste, dried thyme, dried oregano, salt, and pepper. Cook for another 5 minutes, stirring occasionally, until the vegetables are tender and the sauce is slightly thickened. Remove from heat.
5. Transfer the cooked vegetable mixture to the prepared baking dish, spreading it out evenly.
6. Bake in the preheated oven for 20-25 minutes, until the vegetables are tender and the edges are slightly caramelized.
7. Remove from the oven and sprinkle the chopped fresh basil and grated Parmesan cheese (if using) over the top of the casserole.
8. Return the casserole to the oven and bake for an additional 5 minutes, until the cheese is melted and bubbly.

9. Remove from the oven and let it cool for a few minutes before serving.

This ratatouille casserole is a flavorful and nutritious dish that's perfect as a side dish or a main course. It's packed with colorful vegetables and aromatic herbs, creating a delicious and satisfying meal that everyone will love! Enjoy!

Beefy Taco Casserole

Ingredients:

- 1 pound ground beef
- 1 onion, diced
- 1 bell pepper, diced
- 1 packet (1 ounce) taco seasoning mix
- 1 can (15 ounces) black beans, drained and rinsed
- 1 can (15 ounces) corn kernels, drained
- 1 can (10 ounces) diced tomatoes with green chilies, drained
- 1 cup shredded cheddar cheese
- 1 cup shredded Monterey Jack cheese
- 1 cup crushed tortilla chips
- Sour cream, sliced jalapeños, chopped cilantro (for serving, optional)

Instructions:

1. Preheat your oven to 375°F (190°C). Grease a 9x13-inch baking dish with cooking spray.
2. In a large skillet, cook the ground beef over medium heat until browned. Drain excess fat, if any.
3. Add the diced onion and bell pepper to the skillet with the ground beef. Cook until the vegetables are softened, about 5 minutes.
4. Stir in the taco seasoning mix, black beans, corn kernels, and diced tomatoes with green chilies. Cook for another 2-3 minutes, until heated through.
5. Transfer the beef mixture to the prepared baking dish, spreading it out evenly.
6. Sprinkle the shredded cheddar cheese and shredded Monterey Jack cheese evenly over the beef mixture.
7. Sprinkle the crushed tortilla chips evenly over the cheese layer.
8. Cover the baking dish with aluminum foil and bake in the preheated oven for 20 minutes.
9. Remove the foil and bake for an additional 10-15 minutes, or until the cheese is melted and bubbly and the edges are golden brown.
10. Remove from the oven and let it cool for a few minutes before serving.
11. Serve the beefy taco casserole warm, topped with sour cream, sliced jalapeños, and chopped cilantro, if desired.

This beefy taco casserole is a delicious and satisfying dish that's perfect for a family dinner or for entertaining guests. It's packed with flavorful beef, beans, corn, and cheese, all layered together with crunchy tortilla chips for added texture. Enjoy!

Corn and Green Chile Breakfast Casserole

Ingredients:

- 8 large eggs
- 1 cup milk
- 1 can (4 ounces) diced green chilies, drained
- 1 cup frozen corn kernels, thawed
- 1 cup shredded cheddar cheese
- 1 cup shredded Monterey Jack cheese
- 1/2 cup diced red bell pepper
- 1/2 cup diced green bell pepper
- 1/2 cup diced onion
- 1/4 cup chopped fresh cilantro (optional)
- Salt and pepper to taste
- Cooking spray

Instructions:

1. Preheat your oven to 350°F (175°C). Grease a 9x13-inch baking dish with cooking spray.
2. In a large mixing bowl, whisk together the eggs and milk until well combined. Season with salt and pepper to taste.
3. Stir in the diced green chilies, thawed corn kernels, shredded cheddar cheese, shredded Monterey Jack cheese, diced red bell pepper, diced green bell pepper, diced onion, and chopped fresh cilantro (if using). Mix until all ingredients are evenly distributed.
4. Pour the egg mixture into the prepared baking dish, spreading it out evenly.
5. Bake in the preheated oven for 30-35 minutes, or until the eggs are set and the top is golden brown.
6. Remove from the oven and let it cool for a few minutes before serving.
7. Serve the corn and green chile breakfast casserole warm, garnished with additional chopped cilantro if desired.

This corn and green chile breakfast casserole is a flavorful and satisfying dish that's perfect for brunch or breakfast gatherings. It's packed with savory flavors from the green chilies, sweet corn, and colorful bell peppers, making it a delicious and hearty meal to start your day. Enjoy!

Cheesy Broccoli and Rice Casserole

Ingredients:

- 2 cups cooked rice (white or brown)
- 3 cups broccoli florets, steamed until tender
- 1 cup shredded cheddar cheese
- 1 cup shredded mozzarella cheese
- 1/2 cup sour cream
- 1/2 cup mayonnaise
- 1/2 cup milk
- 2 cloves garlic, minced
- 1 teaspoon onion powder
- Salt and pepper to taste
- 1/2 cup grated Parmesan cheese
- Cooking spray

Instructions:

1. Preheat your oven to 350°F (175°C). Grease a 9x13-inch baking dish with cooking spray.
2. In a large mixing bowl, combine the cooked rice, steamed broccoli florets, shredded cheddar cheese, and shredded mozzarella cheese. Mix until well combined.
3. In a separate bowl, whisk together the sour cream, mayonnaise, milk, minced garlic, onion powder, salt, and pepper until smooth.
4. Pour the sour cream mixture over the rice and broccoli mixture in the bowl. Stir until everything is evenly coated.
5. Transfer the mixture to the prepared baking dish, spreading it out evenly.
6. Sprinkle the grated Parmesan cheese evenly over the top of the casserole.
7. Cover the baking dish with aluminum foil and bake in the preheated oven for 25 minutes.
8. Remove the foil and bake for an additional 10-15 minutes, or until the cheese is melted and bubbly and the edges are golden brown.
9. Remove from the oven and let it cool for a few minutes before serving.
10. Serve the cheesy broccoli and rice casserole warm as a delicious side dish or a comforting main course.

This cheesy broccoli and rice casserole is a crowd-pleasing dish that's perfect for family dinners or potlucks. It's creamy, cheesy, and packed with nutritious broccoli and rice, making it a comforting and satisfying meal that everyone will love! Enjoy!

Creamy Chicken and Mushroom Casserole

Ingredients:

- 1.5 pounds boneless, skinless chicken breasts, cut into bite-sized pieces
- Salt and pepper to taste
- 2 tablespoons olive oil
- 8 ounces mushrooms, sliced
- 1 onion, finely chopped
- 3 cloves garlic, minced
- 2 tablespoons all-purpose flour
- 1 cup chicken broth
- 1 cup heavy cream
- 1 teaspoon dried thyme
- 1/2 teaspoon dried rosemary
- 1/2 cup grated Parmesan cheese
- 8 ounces cooked pasta (such as penne or fusilli)
- 1/4 cup chopped fresh parsley, for garnish (optional)

Instructions:

1. Preheat your oven to 375°F (190°C). Grease a 9x13-inch baking dish with cooking spray or butter.
2. Season the chicken pieces with salt and pepper to taste.
3. Heat the olive oil in a large skillet over medium-high heat. Add the seasoned chicken pieces and cook until browned on all sides, about 5-6 minutes. Remove the chicken from the skillet and set aside.
4. In the same skillet, add the sliced mushrooms and cook until they release their moisture and start to brown, about 5 minutes.
5. Add the chopped onion and minced garlic to the skillet with the mushrooms. Cook until the onion is softened and translucent, about 3-4 minutes.
6. Sprinkle the flour over the mushrooms and onions in the skillet. Cook, stirring constantly, for 1-2 minutes to cook off the raw flour taste.
7. Slowly pour in the chicken broth while stirring constantly to prevent lumps from forming. Cook until the mixture thickens, about 2-3 minutes.
8. Stir in the heavy cream, dried thyme, and dried rosemary. Cook for another 2-3 minutes, until the sauce is thick and creamy.

9. Return the cooked chicken pieces to the skillet and stir to coat them evenly with the creamy mushroom sauce.
10. Stir in the grated Parmesan cheese until melted and well combined.
11. Add the cooked pasta to the skillet with the chicken and mushroom mixture. Stir until the pasta is coated with the sauce.
12. Transfer the creamy chicken and mushroom mixture to the prepared baking dish, spreading it out evenly.
13. Bake in the preheated oven for 20-25 minutes, or until the casserole is heated through and bubbly.
14. Remove from the oven and let it cool for a few minutes before serving.
15. Garnish with chopped fresh parsley before serving, if desired.

This creamy chicken and mushroom casserole is a comforting and satisfying dish that's perfect for a cozy family dinner. It's packed with tender chicken, savory mushrooms, and a creamy sauce, making it a delicious and hearty meal that everyone will love! Enjoy!

Vegetarian Eggplant Parmesan Casserole

Ingredients:

- 2 large eggplants, sliced into 1/4-inch rounds
- Salt
- 2 cups marinara sauce
- 2 cups shredded mozzarella cheese
- 1 cup grated Parmesan cheese
- 1 cup breadcrumbs
- 2 tablespoons olive oil
- 2 cloves garlic, minced
- 1 teaspoon dried basil
- 1 teaspoon dried oregano
- Fresh basil leaves, chopped (for garnish)
- Fresh parsley, chopped (for garnish)

Instructions:

1. Preheat your oven to 375°F (190°C). Grease a 9x13-inch baking dish with cooking spray or olive oil.
2. Place the sliced eggplant rounds in a colander and sprinkle generously with salt. Let them sit for about 20-30 minutes to allow excess moisture to drain out.
3. Rinse the salt off the eggplant slices and pat them dry with paper towels.
4. In a shallow dish, mix together the breadcrumbs, grated Parmesan cheese, minced garlic, dried basil, and dried oregano.
5. Dip each eggplant slice into the breadcrumb mixture, coating both sides evenly.
6. Heat the olive oil in a large skillet over medium heat. Cook the breaded eggplant slices in batches until golden brown on both sides, about 3-4 minutes per side. Add more oil as needed.
7. Spread a thin layer of marinara sauce on the bottom of the prepared baking dish.
8. Arrange a layer of the cooked eggplant slices on top of the marinara sauce.
9. Spoon more marinara sauce over the eggplant slices, then sprinkle with shredded mozzarella cheese.
10. Repeat the layers until all the eggplant slices are used, ending with a layer of marinara sauce and shredded mozzarella cheese on top.
11. Cover the baking dish with aluminum foil and bake in the preheated oven for 25 minutes.

12. Remove the foil and bake for an additional 10-15 minutes, or until the cheese is melted and bubbly and the casserole is heated through.
13. Remove from the oven and let it cool for a few minutes before serving.
14. Garnish with chopped fresh basil and parsley before serving, if desired.

This vegetarian eggplant parmesan casserole is a flavorful and satisfying dish that's perfect for a meatless dinner. It's packed with layers of tender eggplant, marinara sauce, and gooey melted cheese, making it a delicious and comforting meal that everyone will love! Enjoy!

Sloppy Joe Tater Tot Casserole

Ingredients:

- 1 pound ground beef
- 1 onion, diced
- 1 green bell pepper, diced
- 1 can (15 ounces) sloppy joe sauce
- 1 can (14.5 ounces) diced tomatoes, drained
- 2 cups shredded cheddar cheese
- 1 bag (32 ounces) frozen tater tots
- Salt and pepper to taste
- Cooking spray

Instructions:

1. Preheat your oven to 375°F (190°C). Grease a 9x13-inch baking dish with cooking spray.
2. In a large skillet, cook the ground beef over medium heat until browned. Drain excess fat.
3. Add the diced onion and green bell pepper to the skillet with the cooked ground beef. Cook until the vegetables are softened, about 5 minutes.
4. Stir in the sloppy joe sauce and diced tomatoes. Season with salt and pepper to taste. Simmer for 5 minutes.
5. Transfer the sloppy joe mixture to the prepared baking dish, spreading it out evenly.
6. Sprinkle the shredded cheddar cheese evenly over the top of the sloppy joe mixture.
7. Arrange the frozen tater tots in a single layer on top of the cheese, covering the entire surface of the casserole.
8. Bake in the preheated oven for 30-35 minutes, or until the tater tots are golden brown and crispy and the cheese is melted and bubbly.
9. Remove from the oven and let it cool for a few minutes before serving.
10. Serve the Sloppy Joe Tater Tot Casserole warm as a delicious and hearty meal.

This Sloppy Joe Tater Tot Casserole is a kid-friendly twist on a classic comfort food dish. It's easy to make and packed with flavor, making it perfect for busy weeknights or family gatherings. Enjoy!

Turkey and Cranberry Casserole

Ingredients:

- 2 cups cooked turkey, shredded or diced
- 1 cup cranberry sauce
- 1 cup cooked stuffing
- 1 cup cooked green beans, chopped
- 1 cup shredded cheddar cheese
- 1/2 cup chicken or turkey broth
- 1/4 cup chopped pecans (optional)
- Salt and pepper to taste
- Cooking spray

Instructions:

1. Preheat your oven to 375°F (190°C). Grease a 9x13-inch baking dish with cooking spray.
2. In a large mixing bowl, combine the cooked turkey, cranberry sauce, cooked stuffing, cooked green beans, shredded cheddar cheese, and chopped pecans (if using). Mix until well combined.
3. Season the mixture with salt and pepper to taste. Stir in the chicken or turkey broth to moisten the ingredients.
4. Transfer the turkey and cranberry mixture to the prepared baking dish, spreading it out evenly.
5. Cover the baking dish with aluminum foil and bake in the preheated oven for 20-25 minutes, or until heated through.
6. Remove the foil and bake for an additional 5-10 minutes, or until the top is golden brown and bubbly.
7. Remove from the oven and let it cool for a few minutes before serving.
8. Serve the Turkey and Cranberry Casserole warm as a delicious and comforting holiday-inspired meal.

This Turkey and Cranberry Casserole is a great way to use up Thanksgiving leftovers or enjoy the flavors of the holiday season any time of year. It's a cozy and satisfying dish that's sure to become a family favorite. Enjoy!

Mexican Beef and Rice Casserole

Ingredients:

- 1 pound ground beef
- 1 onion, diced
- 1 bell pepper, diced
- 2 cloves garlic, minced
- 1 can (14.5 ounces) diced tomatoes, undrained
- 1 can (15 ounces) black beans, drained and rinsed
- 1 cup frozen corn kernels
- 1 cup rice, uncooked
- 2 cups beef broth
- 1 cup shredded cheddar cheese
- 1 teaspoon chili powder
- 1 teaspoon ground cumin
- 1/2 teaspoon paprika
- Salt and pepper to taste
- Chopped fresh cilantro for garnish (optional)
- Sliced avocado for serving (optional)
- Sour cream for serving (optional)

Instructions:

1. Preheat your oven to 375°F (190°C). Grease a 9x13-inch baking dish with cooking spray.
2. In a large skillet, cook the ground beef over medium heat until browned. Drain excess fat.
3. Add the diced onion, bell pepper, and minced garlic to the skillet with the cooked ground beef. Cook until the vegetables are softened, about 5 minutes.
4. Stir in the diced tomatoes, black beans, frozen corn kernels, uncooked rice, beef broth, chili powder, ground cumin, paprika, salt, and pepper. Bring to a simmer.
5. Transfer the mixture to the prepared baking dish, spreading it out evenly.
6. Cover the baking dish with aluminum foil and bake in the preheated oven for 40-45 minutes, or until the rice is cooked and the liquid is absorbed.
7. Remove the foil and sprinkle the shredded cheddar cheese over the top of the casserole.

8. Return the casserole to the oven and bake, uncovered, for an additional 5-10 minutes, or until the cheese is melted and bubbly.
9. Remove from the oven and let it cool for a few minutes before serving.
10. Garnish with chopped fresh cilantro and serve with sliced avocado and sour cream, if desired.

This Mexican Beef and Rice Casserole is a delicious and hearty dish that's perfect for a family dinner. It's packed with flavorful ingredients like ground beef, beans, corn, and spices, all baked together with rice and topped with melted cheese. Enjoy!

Breakfast Sausage and Potato Casserole

Ingredients:

- 1 pound breakfast sausage (pork or turkey), casings removed
- 1 onion, diced
- 2 cloves garlic, minced
- 4 cups frozen hash brown potatoes, thawed
- 1 cup shredded cheddar cheese
- 1 cup shredded mozzarella cheese
- 8 large eggs
- 1/2 cup milk
- 1 teaspoon dried thyme
- Salt and pepper to taste
- Cooking spray

Instructions:

1. Preheat your oven to 375°F (190°C). Grease a 9x13-inch baking dish with cooking spray.
2. In a large skillet, cook the breakfast sausage over medium heat until browned and cooked through, breaking it apart with a spoon as it cooks. Remove the cooked sausage from the skillet and set aside.
3. In the same skillet, add the diced onion and minced garlic. Cook until the onion is softened and translucent, about 3-4 minutes.
4. In a large mixing bowl, combine the cooked sausage, diced onion, minced garlic, thawed hash brown potatoes, shredded cheddar cheese, and shredded mozzarella cheese. Mix until well combined.
5. Transfer the sausage and potato mixture to the prepared baking dish, spreading it out evenly.
6. In a separate bowl, whisk together the eggs, milk, dried thyme, salt, and pepper until well combined.
7. Pour the egg mixture evenly over the sausage and potato mixture in the baking dish.
8. Use a spoon or spatula to gently press down on the mixture to ensure the eggs are evenly distributed.

9. Bake in the preheated oven for 35-40 minutes, or until the eggs are set and the top is golden brown.
10. Remove from the oven and let it cool for a few minutes before serving.
11. Slice into squares and serve warm.

This Breakfast Sausage and Potato Casserole is a hearty and satisfying dish that's perfect for breakfast or brunch. It's packed with savory sausage, tender potatoes, and gooey melted cheese, making it a crowd-pleasing favorite. Enjoy!

Spinach and Feta Pasta Bake

Ingredients:

- 12 ounces pasta (such as penne or rigatoni)
- 2 tablespoons olive oil
- 4 cloves garlic, minced
- 8 cups fresh spinach leaves
- 1 cup crumbled feta cheese
- 1 cup shredded mozzarella cheese
- 1 cup grated Parmesan cheese
- 1 cup ricotta cheese
- 1/2 cup chopped fresh basil
- 1 teaspoon dried oregano
- Salt and pepper to taste
- 1 can (14.5 ounces) diced tomatoes, drained
- 1 can (15 ounces) tomato sauce

Instructions:

1. Preheat your oven to 375°F (190°C). Grease a 9x13-inch baking dish with cooking spray.
2. Cook the pasta according to the package instructions until al dente. Drain and set aside.
3. In a large skillet, heat the olive oil over medium heat. Add the minced garlic and cook until fragrant, about 1 minute.
4. Add the fresh spinach leaves to the skillet and cook until wilted, about 3-4 minutes. Remove from heat.
5. In a large mixing bowl, combine the cooked pasta, wilted spinach, crumbled feta cheese, shredded mozzarella cheese, grated Parmesan cheese, ricotta cheese, chopped fresh basil, dried oregano, salt, and pepper. Mix until well combined.
6. Spread half of the pasta mixture into the prepared baking dish.
7. Spread the diced tomatoes evenly over the pasta mixture in the baking dish.
8. Spread the remaining pasta mixture over the tomatoes.
9. Pour the tomato sauce evenly over the top of the pasta mixture in the baking dish.

10. Cover the baking dish with aluminum foil and bake in the preheated oven for 25 minutes.
11. Remove the foil and bake for an additional 10-15 minutes, or until the cheese is melted and bubbly and the top is golden brown.
12. Remove from the oven and let it cool for a few minutes before serving.
13. Serve the Spinach and Feta Pasta Bake warm, garnished with additional chopped fresh basil if desired.

This Spinach and Feta Pasta Bake is a flavorful and satisfying dish that's perfect for a family dinner or for entertaining guests. It's packed with nutritious spinach, tangy feta cheese, and fragrant basil, all baked together with pasta and tomato sauce for a delicious meal that everyone will love. Enjoy!

BBQ Pulled Pork Mac and Cheese Casserole

Ingredients:

- 12 ounces elbow macaroni
- 2 cups shredded cooked pulled pork
- 1 cup BBQ sauce
- 3 tablespoons butter
- 3 tablespoons all-purpose flour
- 2 cups milk
- 2 cups shredded cheddar cheese
- 1 cup shredded mozzarella cheese
- Salt and pepper to taste
- 1/4 cup breadcrumbs
- Chopped fresh parsley for garnish (optional)

Instructions:

1. Preheat your oven to 375°F (190°C). Grease a 9x13-inch baking dish with cooking spray.
2. Cook the elbow macaroni according to the package instructions until al dente. Drain and set aside.
3. In a large skillet over medium heat, combine the pulled pork and BBQ sauce. Cook, stirring occasionally, until heated through. Remove from heat and set aside.
4. In a separate saucepan, melt the butter over medium heat. Stir in the flour and cook for 1-2 minutes to make a roux.
5. Gradually whisk in the milk, stirring constantly to prevent lumps from forming. Cook until the sauce thickens, about 3-5 minutes.
6. Remove the saucepan from heat and stir in the shredded cheddar cheese and shredded mozzarella cheese until melted and smooth. Season with salt and pepper to taste.
7. In a large mixing bowl, combine the cooked macaroni and cheese sauce, stirring until well coated.
8. Transfer half of the mac and cheese mixture to the prepared baking dish, spreading it out evenly.
9. Spoon the BBQ pulled pork over the mac and cheese layer in the baking dish.

10. Spread the remaining mac and cheese mixture over the pulled pork layer, covering it completely.
11. Sprinkle the breadcrumbs evenly over the top of the casserole.
12. Bake in the preheated oven for 25-30 minutes, or until the top is golden brown and the casserole is bubbly.
13. Remove from the oven and let it cool for a few minutes before serving.
14. Garnish with chopped fresh parsley if desired, and serve warm.

This BBQ Pulled Pork Mac and Cheese Casserole is a delicious and comforting dish that combines the flavors of tender pulled pork with creamy macaroni and cheese, all topped with a crispy breadcrumb crust. It's perfect for a cozy family dinner or for entertaining guests. Enjoy!

Chicken and Dumplings Casserole

Ingredients:

For the Chicken Mixture:

- 2 cups cooked chicken, shredded or diced
- 1 cup frozen mixed vegetables (carrots, peas, corn)
- 1 can (10.5 ounces) cream of chicken soup
- 1/2 cup chicken broth
- 1/2 teaspoon dried thyme
- Salt and pepper to taste

For the Dumplings:

- 1 cup all-purpose flour
- 2 teaspoons baking powder
- 1/2 teaspoon salt
- 1/2 cup milk
- 2 tablespoons melted butter

Instructions:

1. Preheat your oven to 375°F (190°C). Grease a 9x13-inch baking dish with cooking spray.
2. In a large mixing bowl, combine the cooked chicken, frozen mixed vegetables, cream of chicken soup, chicken broth, dried thyme, salt, and pepper. Mix until well combined.
3. Spread the chicken mixture evenly into the prepared baking dish.
4. In another mixing bowl, whisk together the flour, baking powder, and salt for the dumplings.
5. Stir in the milk and melted butter until a thick batter forms.
6. Drop spoonfuls of the dumpling batter onto the chicken mixture in the baking dish, covering it as evenly as possible.
7. Bake in the preheated oven for 25-30 minutes, or until the chicken mixture is bubbly and the dumplings are golden brown on top.

8. Remove from the oven and let it cool for a few minutes before serving.
9. Serve the Chicken and Dumplings Casserole warm as a comforting and satisfying meal.

This Chicken and Dumplings Casserole is a cozy and hearty dish that's perfect for a comforting family dinner. It's packed with tender chicken, mixed vegetables, and fluffy dumplings, all baked together in a creamy sauce. Enjoy!

Mediterranean Chickpea Casserole

Ingredients:

- 2 cans (15 ounces each) chickpeas, drained and rinsed
- 1 onion, finely chopped
- 3 cloves garlic, minced
- 1 bell pepper, diced
- 1 zucchini, diced
- 1 eggplant, diced
- 1 can (14.5 ounces) diced tomatoes
- 1/4 cup chopped fresh parsley
- 1/4 cup chopped fresh basil
- 1 teaspoon dried oregano
- 1 teaspoon dried thyme
- Salt and pepper to taste
- 1/4 cup olive oil
- 1 cup crumbled feta cheese
- 1/4 cup grated Parmesan cheese

Instructions:

1. Preheat your oven to 375°F (190°C). Grease a 9x13-inch baking dish with cooking spray.
2. In a large skillet, heat the olive oil over medium heat. Add the chopped onion and minced garlic, and sauté until softened, about 3-4 minutes.
3. Add the diced bell pepper, zucchini, and eggplant to the skillet. Cook, stirring occasionally, until the vegetables are tender, about 8-10 minutes.
4. Stir in the drained chickpeas, diced tomatoes, chopped parsley, chopped basil, dried oregano, dried thyme, salt, and pepper. Cook for an additional 2-3 minutes to heat through.
5. Transfer the chickpea and vegetable mixture to the prepared baking dish, spreading it out evenly.
6. Sprinkle the crumbled feta cheese and grated Parmesan cheese evenly over the top of the casserole.
7. Cover the baking dish with aluminum foil and bake in the preheated oven for 20 minutes.

8. Remove the foil and bake for an additional 10-15 minutes, or until the cheese is melted and bubbly and the casserole is heated through.
9. Remove from the oven and let it cool for a few minutes before serving.
10. Serve the Mediterranean Chickpea Casserole warm as a flavorful and satisfying vegetarian meal.

This Mediterranean Chickpea Casserole is bursting with vibrant flavors from the fresh vegetables, herbs, and tangy feta cheese. It's a nutritious and delicious dish that's perfect for a meatless dinner option. Enjoy!

Veggie and Quinoa Breakfast Casserole

Ingredients:

- 1 cup quinoa, rinsed
- 2 cups vegetable broth or water
- 1 tablespoon olive oil
- 1 onion, diced
- 2 cloves garlic, minced
- 1 bell pepper, diced
- 1 zucchini, diced
- 1 cup cherry tomatoes, halved
- 1 cup spinach leaves, chopped
- 1 teaspoon dried thyme
- Salt and pepper to taste
- 8 large eggs
- 1/2 cup milk (dairy or non-dairy)
- 1 cup shredded cheese (such as cheddar or mozzarella)
- Fresh herbs for garnish (optional)

Instructions:

1. Preheat your oven to 375°F (190°C). Grease a 9x13-inch baking dish with cooking spray.
2. In a medium saucepan, combine the quinoa and vegetable broth or water. Bring to a boil, then reduce the heat to low, cover, and simmer for 15 minutes, or until the quinoa is cooked and fluffy. Remove from heat and set aside.
3. In a large skillet, heat the olive oil over medium heat. Add the diced onion and minced garlic, and sauté until softened, about 3-4 minutes.
4. Add the diced bell pepper and zucchini to the skillet, and cook for an additional 5 minutes, or until the vegetables are tender.
5. Stir in the halved cherry tomatoes, chopped spinach leaves, dried thyme, salt, and pepper. Cook for another 2-3 minutes, until the spinach is wilted and the tomatoes are slightly softened.
6. In a large mixing bowl, whisk together the eggs and milk until well combined. Season with salt and pepper to taste.

7. Stir in the cooked quinoa and sautéed vegetable mixture into the egg mixture until evenly distributed.
8. Pour the quinoa and vegetable mixture into the prepared baking dish, spreading it out evenly.
9. Sprinkle the shredded cheese evenly over the top of the casserole.
10. Bake in the preheated oven for 25-30 minutes, or until the eggs are set and the cheese is melted and bubbly.
11. Remove from the oven and let it cool for a few minutes before slicing.
12. Garnish with fresh herbs if desired, and serve warm.

This Veggie and Quinoa Breakfast Casserole is nutritious, flavorful, and perfect for a hearty breakfast or brunch. It's loaded with protein-rich quinoa, colorful vegetables, and gooey melted cheese, making it a satisfying and delicious meal to start your day. Enjoy!

www.ingramcontent.com/pod-product-compliance
Lightning Source LLC
LaVergne TN
LVHW081604060526
838201LV00054B/2065